Contents

iv Contents

Access to History

Ger

Britain: Foreign and Imperial Affairs, 1919–39

Alan Farmer

Hodder & Stoughton

LONDON SYDN

The cover illustration is a portrait of Neville Chamberlain by Henry Lamb, c1939 (Courtesy National Portrait Gallery)

Some other titles in the series:

Britain: Domestic Politics, 1918–39   ISBN 0 340 55647 1
Robert Pearce

Labour and Reform: Working Class Movements, 1815–1914   ISBN 0 340 52930 X
Clive Behagg

The Concert of Europe: International Relations, 1814–70 ISBN 0 340 53496 6
John Lowe

Rivalry and Accord: International Relations, 1870–1914   ISBN 0 340 51806 5
John Lowe

Italy: Liberalism and Fascism, 1870–1945   ISBN 0 340 54548 8
Mark Robson

Germany: The Third Reich, 1933–45   ISBN 0 340 53047 3
Geoff Layton

British Library Cataloguing in Publication Data

Farmer, Alan
  Britain: Foreign and Imperial Affairs,
  1919–45. – (Access to History Series)
  I. Title II. Series
  941.083

  ISBN 0–340–55928–4

First published 1992

© 1992 Alan Farmer

Typeset by Wearset, Boldon, Tyne and Wear
Printed in Great Britain for the educational publishing division of
Hodder & Stoughton Ltd, Mill Road, Dunton Green, Sevenoaks, Kent
by Page Bros. (Norwich) Ltd

Contents v

Preface

To the general reader

Although the *Access to History* series has been designed with the needs of students studying the subject at higher examination levels very much in mind, it also has a great deal to offer the general reader. The main body of the text (i.e. ignoring the Study Guides at the ends of chapters) forms a readable and yet stimulating survey of a coherent topic as studied by historians. However, each author's aim has not merely been to provide a clear explanation of what happened in the past (to interest and inform): it has also been assumed that most readers wish to be stimulated into thinking further about the topic and to form opinions of their own about the significance of the events that are described and discussed (to be challenged). Thus, although no prior knowledge of the topic is expected on the reader's part, she or he is treated as an intelligent and thinking person throughout. The author tends to share ideas and possibilities with the reader, rather than passing on numbers of so-called 'historical truths'.

To the student reader

There are many ways in which the series can be used by students studying History at a higher level. It will, therefore, be worthwhile thinking about your own study strategy before you start your work on this book. Obviously, your strategy will vary depending on the aim you have in mind, and the time for study that is available to you.

If, for example, you want to acquire a general overview of the topic in the shortest possible time, the following approach will probably be the most effective:

1 Read chapter 1 and think about its contents.
2 Read the 'Making notes' section at the end of chapter 2 and decide whether it is necessary for you to read this chapter.
3 Repeat stage 2 (and stage 3 where appropriate) for all the other chapters.

If, however, your aim is to gain a thorough grasp of the topic, taking however much time is necessary to do so, you may benefit from carrying out the same procedure with each chapter, as follows:

1 Read the chapter as fast as you can, and preferably at one sitting.
2 Study the flow diagram at the end of the chapter, ensuring that you understand the general 'shape' of what you have just read.
3 Read the 'Making notes' section (and the 'Answering essay

questions' section, if there is one) and decide what further work you
need to do on the chapter.

4   Attempt the 'Source-based questions' section. It will sometimes
be sufficient to think through your answers, but additional understanding will often be gained by forcing yourself to write them
down.

When you have finished the main chapters of the book, study the
'Further Reading' section and decide what additional reading (if any)
you will do on the topic.

This book has been designed to help make your studies both
enjoyable and successful. If you can think of ways in which this could
have been done more effectively, please write to tell me. In the
meantime, I hope that you will gain greatly from your study of History.

Keith Randell

CHAPTER 1

Introduction: Peace-making and Policy-making

1 Britain's Position in 1919

In November 1918, after four years of savage conflict, an armistice finally brought the First World War – or Great War – to an end. In Britain, as in other victorious countries, there was great rejoicing and hope of a golden era of peace and prosperity. Lloyd George, the Prime Minister, talked of Britain becoming a 'land fit for heroes'.

Britain seemed to have emerged from the First World War in an immensely strong position. She had not suffered devastation, unlike much of Belgium and parts of northern France. She had lost only 5 per cent of her active male population, whereas France had lost 10 per cent and Germany 15 per cent. In 1918 Britain seemed the greatest power in the victorious alliance. Her mobilisation of resources was at its peak. She ended the war with an army of 5,500,000 men; the navy had 58 capital (battle) ships, over 100 cruisers, and a host of lesser craft; the airforce had over 20,000 planes. Both national and Empire solidarity had held firm throughout the war. The British Empire, which amounted to nearly one quarter of the world's land surface, had greatly assisted the mother country's war effort, providing vital raw materials and some 2,500,000 'colonial' troops. The war seemed to provide proof of the Empire's unity and utility.

Britain's position was enhanced by the weakness of its traditional rivals. Germany, the main threat to Britain before 1914, was defeated; her army had ceased to exist as a major fighting force; her fleet was in the hands of the British at Scapa Flow; her empire was lost; and her economy seemed near collapse. Russia, Britain's ally in the First World War but a rival for much of the nineteenth century, was in chaos. A Bolshevik government, led by Lenin, had seized power in November 1917 but was now under attack from 'White' Russian forces, backed by various Allied powers, including Britain. The Russian economy was in tatters and several provinces had taken advantage of the turmoil to declare their independence from Russia.

Britain seemed to have little to fear from the other great powers which had emerged victorious from the war. France had been hard hit by the war and needed British friendship against Germany. Although the USA and Japan were now much stronger, neither seemed likely to pose an immediate challenge. America had aligned itself decisively with Britain in the War and common ties of language, culture and tradition meant that there was already talk of a 'special relationship' between the two Anglo-Saxon powers. Britain was also on good terms with Japan.

The two countries had been allied since 1902 and the alliance had held throughout the War.

The economic impact of the First World War was less considerable than many had feared. Britain's enormous reserves of wealth and its established hold on many overseas markets cushioned the blow. There was no great trade deficit: indeed the balance of payments remained in the black for the war years as a whole. The elimination of German competition helped British manufacturers. The great industrial effort of the war seemed to have demonstrated the strength and flexibility of the British economy. In spite of millions of men being mobilised for the armed forces, industrial output had hardly fallen. So healthy was the economy that Britain had been able to pay for the war largely out of her own resources and had even been able to loan vast sums of money to other Allied governments, especially Russia. Although Britain did owe money to the USA, most of this debt had been contracted by Britain on behalf of her Allies, who owed Britain far more money than she owed America.

In 1919 most Britons assumed that the Great War had been the war to end wars. Few envisaged that two decades later their country would become involved in a Second World War and that when this war ended Britain would no longer be a first class world power. So what went wrong? Why did a second war have to be fought and why did Britain's relative international position decline so sharply?

Historians have placed emphasis on different factors to explain Britain's decline between 1919 and 1945. Some think that the Second World War had a massive effect on Britain's international position. They see Britain as a first rate power in 1939. They see the war as 'instigating' Britain's decline. Some claim that if Britain had not gone to war in 1939 she might well have maintained much of her pre-war status. These historians have a tendency to criticise the British statesmen of the period. Lloyd George and the other main peacemakers of 1919 have frequently been condemned. The flawed Treaty of Versailles is often seen as sowing the seeds of the Second World War. Others have blamed the 'appeasers' of the 1930s – especially Neville Chamberlain.

However, other historians have claimed that, given the realities of the modern world, Britain's decline was almost inevitable, whoever was in power and whatever they did. They argue that Britain was already in retreat before 1914 and that this retreat continued through the inter-war years. They regard the Second World War as a catalyst – an accelerator of already established trends. Given the weaknesses of Britain's position, they tend to have more sympathy with the inter-war statesmen. However, few historians of the 'catalyst' school would accept that events in history are inevitable. Therefore most would accept that the policies of individual statesmen did have considerable effect. Governments cannot necessarily escape blame for their actions. But perhaps it is wrong to talk about blame. Perhaps most – if not all –

governments and statesmen acted for good and rational reasons. Perhaps Britain's position in 1945 might have been worse – but for their actions!

The debates about who was responsible for the Second World War and who – or what – was responsible for Britain's decline are likely to go on. Two of the debates – the efficacy (or otherwise!) of the Treaty of Versailles, and consideration of Britain's problems in facing up to the challenges of the modern world – will be examined in this chapter. The actions of British governments and statesmen from 1919–39 make up the rest of the book.

2 The Treaty of Versailles

a) The Aims of the Peacemakers

When Germany had sought peace terms in the autumn of 1918 she had assumed these would be based on President Woodrow Wilson's Fourteen Points. These had been contained in an address to the American Congress in January 1918. Wilson, seeking to distance himself from traditional European diplomatic dealings, had talked in terms of a peace based on justice, equality and democracy. He had later stated that the eventual peace should contain 'no annexations, no contributions, no punitive damages'. Wilson's Fourteen Points (later amplified by the Four Principles and Five Particulars) were regarded as idealistic pipedreams by most hard-headed European statesmen. But they could not be rejected out of hand. If they were to defeat Germany, Britain and France had to retain the support of the USA, the world's strongest economic power. However both Lloyd George, the British Prime Minister, and Georges Clemenceau, the French leader, did express serious reservations about some of Wilson's ideas. They were aware that most people in Britain and France wanted a harsh peace. By November 1918 even Wilson accepted that Germany should make compensation 'for all damage done to the civilian population of the Allies'.

The peace conference which assembled in Paris in January 1919 was dominated by the Big Three – Lloyd George, Clemenceau and Wilson. All had impeccable liberal credentials. They each took their job seriously and each had large supporting teams of experts. All three were concerned with the main question: how to provide security for the future. But all held very different views, in part reflecting the popular pressure to which they were subjected.

Clemenceau was determined on a punitive peace. Twice in his lifetime France had been invaded by Germany. In 1871 she had lost Alsace-Lorraine and been forced to pay massive reparations. French casualties between 1914 and 1918 were the highest sustained by the Allied powers. Clemenceau, 'The Tiger', wanted German power reduced so that all prospect of a future military threat was eliminated. In demanding security and compensation for the losses France had endured, he was asking no more than every Frenchman expected.

Woodrow Wilson was less interested in punishing Germany. America faced no immediate military threat and had no territorial or even overt economic aims. Wilson came to the peace conference still affirming general principles. He was primarily concerned with establishing an equitable and lasting system of international relations. In particular he wanted to set up a League of Nations and favoured the principle of self-determination for all subject peoples.

Lloyd George's position is more difficult to define. Although Britain had no territorial claims in Europe, Lloyd George was anxious to preserve Britain's naval supremacy and also prepared (under Conservative pressure) to enlarge the British Empire – time-honoured British objectives. Aware of the strong anti-German feeling in Britain, he had announced in the 1918 election campaign that he expected Germany to pay 'to the limit of her capacity' for the damage she had inflicted. Lloyd George was prepared to destroy German militarism and even support demands that Kaiser Wilhelm II should be hung. However he distinguished between the old imperial German leaders and the German people as a whole. Germany was now ruled by parliamentary leaders. It seemed unwise to undermine their authority or to persecute them for the sins of the Kaiser. Conscious of the danger of leaving an embittered Germany, he was inclined to leniency. In his Fontainbleu memorandum of March 1919 he wrote:

1 I cannot imagine any greater cause for future war than that the
   German people who have proved themselves one of the most
   powerful and vigorous races of the world, should be surrounded
   by a number of small states, many of them consisting of peoples
5 who have never previously set up a stable government for
   themselves, but each containing large masses of Germans cla-
   mouring for reunion with their native land . . . You may strip
   Germany of her colonies, reduce her armaments to a mere police
   force and her navy to that of a fifth rate power; all the same in the
10 end if she feels that she has been unjustly treated in the peace of
   1919 she will find means of exacting retribution.

Lloyd George also feared that if Germany was excessively humiliated she might be driven into the arms of the Bolsheviks. While he talked 'hard' for home consumption, he was to act 'soft' and do all he could to ease some of the harsher terms that Clemenceau was intent on imposing.

Lloyd George had critics at the time – and since. J.M. Keynes, the famous economist, portrayed him as a political chameleon, 'rooted in nothing', 'void and without content'. He has been attacked for ignoring the views of his Cabinet colleagues and for refusing to delegate. Some historians have concluded that his principal aim at Versailles was simply to win popularity at home. Others have argued that he was devious, unscrupulous and delighted in improvisation; so much so that the means justified themselves almost irrespective of the ends.

However Lloyd George also had and has his supporters. Some regard him as the most inspired and creative British statesman of the twentieth century. Many more see him as charting a tricky – and skilful – course between the opposing views of Clemenceau and Wilson, while at the same time trying (with considerable success) to preserve British interests. His defenders claim that he, of all the peace-makers, had the most realistic and idealistic post-war vision to reinforce his spell-binding skills as a negotiator.

Lloyd George has often been seen as the main architect of the Versailles settlement. It is claimed that he was in a strong position because he often found himself able to mediate between Clemenceau and Wilson. However, this is a debateable claim. Many historians have viewed Lloyd George, rather than Wilson, as the opponent of most of the extreme French demands. Thus the American President could be seen as being in the best bargaining position. The records seem to suggest that the process of bargaining among the Big Three was highly complex, with attitudes by no means fixed. Certainly the final treaty was the result of a whole series of compromises on many issues. It would be wrong, therefore, to single out Lloyd George as the main arbiter of the peace settlement.

b) The Main Terms of the Treaty of Versailles

i) Territorial Changes

Negotiations about Germany's frontiers, both in the east and west, were highly contentious. The French at first demanded that the western frontier of Germany should be fixed on the River Rhine. The area on the left bank would go to France or become an independent buffer state. Lloyd George and Wilson both opposed this idea, believing it would become a cause of constant German resentment. Clemenceau pressed hard but failed to get his way. He was appeased by the promise of an Anglo-American defensive guarantee. It was also agreed that Germany should return Alsace-Lorraine to France and Eupen and Malmedy to Belgium. Though the Rhineland was not divorced from Germany, it was to be occupied by Allied troops for 15 years and was to remain permanently demilitarised. The Saar region was placed under League of Nations control for 15 years, during which time the French could work its coal mines. A plebiscite would then be held to decide the area's future.

The settlement of Germany's eastern border caused even more

Key:

- ▨ Lost by Germany 1919
- ◼ Saar: League of Nations control
- ▥ Demilitarized Rhineland
- ▤ Austria–Hungary until 1918
- ▨ Plebiscite areas
- ▥ Former territory of imperial Russia

Scale: 0 — 200 mls / 0 — 200 km

FINLAND

NORWAY

SWEDEN

ESTONIA

North Sea

Baltic Sea

LATVIA

DENMARK

Memel • LITHUANIA

Northern Schleswig

USSR

HOLLAND

Danzig (Free City)

EAST PRUSSIA

BELGIUM

Berlin •

POLAND

Eupen Malmédy

GERMANY

Warsaw •

Silesia

LUX. SAAR

Alsace-Lorraine

Prague • CZECHOSLOVAKIA

Munich •

Vienna •

FRANCE

AUSTRIA

• Budapest

HUNGARY

BESSARABIA

SWITZERLAND

Fiume

Belgrade

RUMANIA

YUGOSLAVIA

CROATIA

ITALY

Adriatic Sea

SERBIA

BULGARIA

MONTENEGRO

ALBANIA

TURKEY

GREECE

Mediterranean Sea

The Versailles Peace Settlement

problems. The Fourteen Points had promised to create an independent Poland which would be given free and secure access to the sea. Germany could, therefore, expect to lose land to Poland. However, it was difficult to determine which land this should be because there was no clear-cut division between areas of German and Polish majority population in eastern Germany. The French wanted a strong Poland and supported the most extreme Polish territorial claims. But Lloyd George, fearful of incorporating millions of embittered Germans within the new state, fought to keep Poland as small as possible. It was because of his pressure that the key port of Danzig was made a Free City under the League of Nations and that a plebiscite was held (in 1921) in Upper Silesia, with the result that only about one third of the area went to Poland. But the final territorial settlement in the east satisfied no one. The Germans were outraged by the loss of land to Poland, especially the loss of the Polish corridor which separated East Prussia from the rest of Germany. Germany also lost Memel to Lithuania, and was forbidden to unite with the Germanic 'rump' state of Austria. Had she been allowed to do so this would have enhanced Germany's pre-war power. However, this decision merely reinforced the belief that the peace-makers had made up their minds that the principle of self-determination would not be applied to Germans.

Germany also lost all her colonies. Britain gained German East Africa and the Cameroons; Australia took New Guinea; South Africa acquired South-West Africa; New Zealand got Samoa; and Japan took all German possessions in China and in the Pacific north of the Equator. On Wilson's insistence, these areas were to be ruled as mandates. This meant that the ruling powers had to bear in mind the wishes of the colonial inhabitants who should eventually be prepared for self-government under the supervision of the League of Nations. Lloyd George was not opposed to this principle which he described as 'virtually a codification of existing British practice'. The main opposition to the idea of mandated territory came from the Dominions and Japan, who favoured outright annexation!

ii) Armaments
The Allies agreed that German military power should be severely reduced. Germany was to have no heavy artillery, tanks or aeroplanes, and her army was limited to 100,000 men. She was to have no capital ships and no submarines. An Allied Control Commission was set up to police these arrangements.

iii) Reparations and War Guilt
Article 231 of the Treaty of Versailles stated that:

1 The Allied and Associated Governments affirm and Germany accepts the responsibility of Germany and her allies for all the loss

to which the Allied and Associated Governments and their
nationals have been subjected as a consequence of the war
5 imposed upon them by the aggression of Germany and her allies.

This so-called War Guilt clause provided a moral basis for the Allied
demands for Germany to pay reparations. In reality, the clause, which
was hated by the Germans, had little practical effect as the Germans had
already accepted in the terms of the Armistice that they would make
compensation for 'all damage done to the civilian population of the
Allies'. The main difficulty was deciding how much Germany could and
should pay, and how this money should be divided among the Allies.
Wilson wanted a reparations settlement based on Germany's ability to
pay. However, the French and British publics wanted, in the words of
Sir Auckland Geddes, 'to squeeze the German lemon till the pips
squeaked'. This would serve the dual purpose of helping the Allied
countries meet the cost of the war and also keep Germany financially
weak for years to come. Lloyd George was pulled several ways. He was
determined that Britain should get her fair share of reparations and
insisted (successfully) that 'damage' should include merchant shipping
losses and the costs of pensions to those disabled, widowed or orphaned
by the war. Like Wilson, however, he thought that Germany should
only pay what she could reasonably afford and he was impressed by the
view that if Germany was hit too hard she would no longer be a good
market for British goods – which would damage the post-war British
economy. However, whatever his own feelings, Lloyd George could not
afford to ignore the prevailing mood in Britain or the fact that in the
1918 election, he himself had promised to screw Germany 'to the
uttermost farthing'.
    Astronomical reparation figures were bandied about. In the end, at
Lloyd George's suggestion, a Reparations Commission was set up to
determine the amount. This effectively postponed an immediate decision and allowed tempers to cool. In 1921 the Reparations Commission
finally recommended a sum of £6,600,000 million. Although this was
far less than originally envisaged, some economists and most Germans
claimed (probably wrongly) that it was more than Germany could
afford.

iv) The League of Nations
The League of Nations was written into the Treaty of Versailles. This
was Woodrow Wilson's obsession. He had believed (quite wrongly) that
Britain and France would oppose the idea of the League. Although
neither Lloyd George nor Clemenceau were enthusiastic advocates,
both were prepared to support the concept of the League in return for
the friendship of the USA. Indeed the British Foreign Office, inspired
by Lord Robert Cecil (Deputy Foreign Secretary) and Jan Smuts
(South African Minister of Defence) had prepared a concrete scheme

for the League, whereas the Americans had come to Paris 'armed' only with rather vague and woolly ideas. The British scheme became the framework for the League of Nations. The Allies had different views about the way that the League should operate but they all agreed that Germany should not be allowed to join until she had given solid proof of her intention to carry out the peace terms.

The treaty was completed in great haste at the end of April 1919 and when it was rushed to the printers nobody had actually read the 440 clauses in full! The Germans, allowed only three weeks to make written observations, attacked nearly every provision, especially the War Guilt, reparations and territorial clauses. In the end, however, Germany had no option but to accept the treaty or face the threat of invasion. The Treaty of Versailles was finally signed on 28 June 1919.

3 Criticisms of Versailles

In 1919 the Treaty of Versailles was well received in Britain and passed through parliament with overwhelming majorities. On the whole Britain seemed to have gained what she wanted from the peace settlement. German naval power had been destroyed (the German fleet scuttled itself in Scapa Flow in June 1919). Britain and her Dominions had acquired German colonies and Germany had agreed to pay reparations. The prevailing British view was that the treaty was firm but just.

This was not the prevailing view in Germany. Germans of all political persuasions claimed that the treaty was punitive and unfair, and a major departure from Wilson's Fourteen Points which they had been led to believe would be the basis of the peace settlement. Radical opinion in Britain soon reached the same conclusion. In 1919 the economist J.M. Keynes wrote a devastating critique of the treaty in an influential book, *The Economic Consequences of the Peace*. He argued that a naive Wilson had been forced by a vindictive Clemenceau and the scheming Lloyd George to agree to an over-harsh peace. He particularly condemned the undesirability and unworkability of the reparations clauses. Even Lloyd George had doubts about the treaty and suspected that Germany had been treated unfairly. These doubts were to be echoed by many other British politicians in the years ahead.

However, most Frenchmen considered the treaty far too soft. After a long and costly war, for which she was largely responsible, Germany had lost only 13 per cent of her pre-war territory and 10 per cent of her population. She had escaped division, was now surrounded only by small, unstable states on her southern and eastern borders, and remained potentially the strongest state in Europe. Clemenceau had been prepared to accept the Versailles terms only because Wilson and Lloyd George had offered France a defensive alliance. The American Senate, however, refused to ratify this guarantee and the British government then did likewise. Most Frenchmen, in consequence, felt betrayed.

Historians have generally echoed these contemporary criticisms. Many have claimed that the treaty was the worst of all worlds – too severe to be permanently acceptable to most Germans, and too lenient to constrain Germany for long, particularly without effective enforcement. Some historians, such as A.J.P. Taylor, have gone as far as to claim that it was the Allies' failure to solve the German problem in 1919 that laid the foundation of the Second World War.

However, not all historians have been so critical and some (such as Kennedy and Adamthwaite) have been prepared to defend both the peacemakers and the treaty. They have stressed the problems that Lloyd George and his fellow peace-makers faced in 1919. While they have agreed that the German problem was not solved, they have pointed out that, even with hindsight, it is difficult to suggest realistic solutions to that problem. They have claimed that the overriding problem was not so much the terms of Versailles, but rather German hostility to the treaty because it represented a defeat which most Germans were not willing to acknowledge. Even a treaty based on the Fourteen Points would not have been acceptable to Germany because it would have involved the loss of land to Poland. A really severe treaty was out of the question given Wilson's and Lloyd George's desire for a just settlement. In the circumstances Adamthwaite sees Versailles as a 'brave attempt to deal with intractable, perhaps insoluble problems'.

The Big Three, jumping from question to question and under severe domestic pressures, were not unaware of the deficiencies in their handiwork. But this was precisely why, so far as Lloyd George was concerned, the League of Nations was created. In 1919 he said that it would 'be there as a Court of Appeal to readjust crudities, irregularities, injustices'. This was perhaps putting too much faith in an organisation which lacked enforcement powers. Moreover (and Lloyd George did not realise this in 1919), the League was also to lack America! The American Senate refused to ratify the Treaty of Versailles and thus the USA did not become a member of the League. The result, according to Medlicott, was that 'Britain and France were left as the embarrassed nursemaids of a rather endearing spastic infant, the product of some injudicious international love making'(!)

4 Problems Facing British Statesmen in the Inter-war Years

Some historians would lay the responsibility for the Second World War with the statesmen who came after 1919, rather than with Lloyd George and the others who drew up the peace treaty. The British Prime Ministers between the wars, Bonar Law, Stanley Baldwin, Ramsay MacDonald and Neville Chamberlain, are often seen as lightweights, a lesser breed than the two war leaders Lloyd George and Winston

Churchill. They are criticised for pursuing conciliatory, 'safety first' policies. Stanley Baldwin and Neville Chamberlain have been particularly condemned for their attempts to 'appease' Germany. After the Second World War Winston Churchill's view, that Britain should have stood up to Hitler much sooner, carried – and indeed still carries – great weight.

However, many recent historians have treated the inter-war statesmen with far more sympathy and, in particular, have stressed the problems they faced. These problems were such that efforts to preserve both peace and Britain's status would probably have been unavailing, even had great statesmanship been displayed in London.

Britain's influential position in world affairs in the nineteenth century was due to a number of inter-related factors. The Industrial Revolution had ensured that Britain was both the workshop and banking house of the world before 1870. Throughout the eighteenth and nineteenth centuries the British navy had ruled the waves, ensuring that Britain was secure from attack. Economic and naval supremacy had helped Britain acquire the most extensive empire the world had ever seen. However, by 1900 Britain's economic position was threatened by Germany and the USA, which had become serious industrial rivals. By the early years of the twentieth century Germany even seemed to pose a potential military threat.

By 1919 Germany was defeated. However, the First World War, far from boosting Britain's economic position, had imposed serious strain. The financial costs had been massive – £7,000,000 a day, only paid for by heavy borrowing. There was an elevenfold increase in the National Debt, the annual interest payments of which consumed a large percentage of central government expenditure in the inter-war years. Moreover Britain had been forced to sell off some of her overseas investments, which had a damaging effect on the country's balance of payments. To make matters worse, the war had damaged Britain's industrial capacity. In many cases normal replacement and improvement of industrial plant and machinery had been postponed. She had also lost many lucrative markets, especially in Latin America and the Far East, to America and Japan. As a consequence, the British economy stuttered through the inter-war years. Even in the 1920s British manufacturers had a poor export record and there was a high rate of unemployment. The world-wide depression of the 1930s further rocked the economy. Britain's share of world trade steadily declined.

Britain's economic difficulties had foreign policy repercussions as there were clear limits to the amount Britain could afford to spend on defence. Unlike the USA, she could not ignore developments in Europe, and she was also a great imperial power with global commitments. Many on both the right and the left saw her as the policeman of the world. Those on the right believed Britain could and should maintain British interests wherever and whenever they were challenged. Those on the left thought Britain should enforce the decisions of the League of Nations. Indeed at no time in the inter-war years could ministers free themselves from the popular assumption that on them rested the responsibility for defending the victims of aggression in any part of the world. But economic and financial weakness meant there was a growing disparity between Britain's world-wide commitments and her capacity to meet them.

Britain could not even rely on others to help her police-keeping role. The First World War alliance with France soon wore thin. In 1921 Lord Curzon wrote that 'in almost every quarter of the globe . . . the representatives of France are actively pursuing a policy which is either unfriendly to British interests or, if not that, is consecrated to the promotion of a French interest which is inconsistent with ours'. Indeed in some quarters there was a fear of an over-strong France which might pursue Napoleonic dreams of empire.

The USA emerged from the First World War as potentially the world's greatest power. Indeed, without American financial, economic and ultimately military help it is unlikely that Britain and France would have won the war. But after 1919 the USA was reluctant to involve herself in European, or indeed world, affairs, especially in the 1930s when her assistance was most needed. Most American Presidents were not indifferent to Europe (and Asia), but their willingness and ability to exert themselves was severely constrained by the political and economic situation within the USA. Many British politicians hoped for a closer co-operation with America, but British governments soon recognised that they could not base their foreign policy upon it. In 1932 Baldwin said, 'You will get nothing from America but words: big words but only words'. Only the Japanese attack on Pearl Harbour in 1941 forced the USA to end her, not always 'splendid', isolation.

Nor could Britain depend on her empire, which was not as strong as it seemed. There were growing nationalist movements in many parts of it, especially in India – the 'jewel in the crown'. Even the Dominions – especially South Africa, Canada and (after 1922) the Irish Free State – were anxious to achieve greater autonomy and to develop their own separate foreign policies, rather than be committed, even with prior consultation, to the consequences of British diplomacy.

British statesmen also had to face the fact that several potentially very strong nations had grievances and ambitions that might well threaten world peace and even Britain's security. Germany, Russia, Italy and Japan, for a variety of reasons, were dissatisfied with both the peace settlement and the status quo.

After 1918 British statesmen no longer had quite the same room for manoeuvre in foreign affairs as their counterparts in earlier generations. The 1918 general election in Britain was the first to be conducted on the basis of full manhood suffrage and there was also a limited franchise for women. Politicians could now gain and preserve power only by winning the support of a far larger electorate than in the past. In consequence, public opinion had a far greater influence on foreign policy than ever before. For example, British governments throughout most of the inter-war years could not ignore the deep-seated yearning for peace on the part of the electorate. Most voters thought that money should be spent on domestic matters and social reform, rather than on armaments and adventures abroad. Developments in communications – newspapers, radio and cinema – meant that statesmen now negotiated in the full glare of publicity. Day to day dealings with foreign countries were subject to much greater scrutiny, sometimes with disastrous effects on difficult and delicate negotiations.

5 British Interests

British statesmen responded to the difficulties they faced in different ways. Ministers in Labour governments, for example, were more prepared to come to terms with the USSR and professed a greater faith in disarmament and the League of Nations than Conservative ministers. The Conservative Party, in power for most of the period 1919–39, was never fully united on foreign or imperial affairs. Some Conservatives, like Winston Churchill, favoured Britain taking a firm stand against Hitler's Germany. Others supported the policy of appeasing Hitler.

But, although there were differences of emphasis, most governments throughout the inter-war period (whether Conservative or Labour) tended to adopt similar policies. In part, this reflected the general political situation. On the two occasions when the Labour Party was in power (1924 and 1929–31) it depended on Liberal support and was more moderate than would have been suggested by the tone of Labour MPs' speeches when in opposition. Although there were divisions in the Conservative Party, an overwhelming majority of its MPs supported the policies of Stanley Baldwin and Neville Chamberlain, rather than those of Winston Churchill who was in the political wilderness for most of the 1930s. Given the fact that the Liberal vote remained quite strong throughout the inter-war years, both the Conservative and Labour Parties tended to appeal to the middle ground, with the result that there was consensus politics. This was particularly true in the 1930s, when National Governments were in power. These were dominated by the Conservatives, but included both Labour and Liberal MPs.

Throughout this period there was also strong continuity in the personnel and assumptions of most professional diplomats and Foreign Office officials. Nearly all were from similar backgrounds – public school and Oxbridge. Many held their posts for a long time. Their experience and expertise gave the officials considerable influence over most prime ministers and foreign secretaries. This helped to ensure a certain continuity in style and purpose. Prudence, pragmatism, mod-

BRITISH GOVERNMENTS, PRIME MINISTERS
AND FOREIGN SECRETARIES 1919–39

GOVERN-MENTS		PRIME MINISTERS	FOREIGN SECRETARIES
War Cabinet	Dec. 1916–Jan. 1919	D. Lloyd George	A.J. Balfour
Coalition	Jan. 1919–Oct. 1922	D. Lloyd George	A.J. Balfour (until Oct. 1919) then Lord Curzon
Conservative	Oct. 1922–May 1923	A. Bonar Law	Lord Curzon
Conservative	May 1923–Jan. 1924	Stanley Baldwin	Lord Curzon
Labour	Jan. 1924–Nov. 1924	Ramsay MacDonald	Ramsay MacDonald
Conservative	Nov. 1924–June 1929	Stanley Baldwin	Austen Chamberlain
Labour	June 1929–Aug. 1931	Ramsay MacDonald	Arthur Henderson
National	Aug. 1931–June 1935	Ramsay MacDonald	Marquess of Reading (until Dec. 1935) then Sir John Simon
National (Conservative)	June 1935–May 1937	Stanley Baldwin	Sir Samuel Hoare (until Dec. 1935) then Anthony Eden
National (Conservative)	May 1937–May 1940	Neville Chamberlain	Anthony Eden (until Mar. 1938) then Lord Halifax

eration, a tendency to understatement and irony; all tended to be features of the British government's style, almost regardless of which party was in power. Therefore most prime ministers and foreign secretaries throughout the period tended to pursue similar aims. A secret Foreign Office memorandum in April 1926 described Britain's main concerns:

1 We have got all that we want – perhaps more. Our sole object is to keep what we have and live in peace. Many foreign countries are playing for a definite stake and their policy is shaped accordingly. It is not so in our case. To the casual observer our foreign policy
5 may appear to lack consistency and continuity, but both are there. We keep our hands free in order to throw our weight into the scale and on behalf of peace. The maintenance of the balance of power and the preservation of the status quo have been our guiding lights for many decades and will so continue.

Peace seemed the greatest of national interests. The scale of the bloodshed in the Great War made both politicians and public recoil from the prospect of a new war. For most of the inter-war period (until 1939) no electoral advantage could be gained by waving the flag and beating the drum. Peace helped promote commerce, essential to British prosperity. There was also an awareness that Britain was increasingly vulnerable to new weapons of war. Submarines could threaten the navy, so long the shield of Britain, while aircraft could attack British cities, however strong the navy. Britain seemed to have everything to lose and nothing to gain from a major war.

Most British governments wished to maintain the balance of power in Europe as the best insurance against the renewal of war. But most were also reluctant to assume any definite commitments in the furtherance of this aim. Many Britons now bitterly resented the fact that the First World War, arising from an obscure Balkan quarrel, had dragged in western nations because of a rigid alliance system and fixed military plans. As a result, most British governments had no intention of binding the country to preserve the status quo – in particular, the new, questionable boundaries of eastern Europe. This was to remain a cardinal tenet of British policy until 1939.

Most politicians appreciated the importance of Europe to Britain, but very few considered Britain a fully-fledged European state. British interests were global rather than just continental. It was thought that the preservation of the Empire was essential if Britain was to remain a great world power. Although most politicians claimed that self-government was the ultimate destiny of every part of the empire, there was determination within Britain to preserve the imperial union in some form.

Another key aim was to remain on good terms with the USA. Britain, as all administrations realised, could not afford even a minor quarrel with America. The USA was already a great economic power and was also potentially a great military power. Britain might well need her assistance in the future, just as she had needed her assistance in the First World War. A permanent quarrel with America was unthinkable.

A vital concern of all governments was to ensure that Britain was adequately defended. Defence policy was based on four main objectives: the security of the United Kingdom; the protection of essential British trade routes; defence of the empire; and a readiness to co-operate in the defence of Britain's allies. Throughout the period British governments had to assess Britain's defence requirements in the light of the current international situation and in terms of what the country could afford. Until the 1930s it was the policy of successive governments to keep defence spending as low as possible, and to promote disarmament whenever they could.

After 1919 Britain's army was massively cut. It rapidly reverted to its pre-war role of imperial police force. The navy, although treated less harshly, also suffered. Agreements with Britain's naval competitors ensured that there were no replacement battleships. Cruisers and destroyers were steadily reduced. Naval stores were run down and Britain's string of bases throughout the world was neglected – with the exception of Singapore. The RAF preserved its separate identity but remained small in size. However, there was a growing belief in the effect of the bomber deterrent. Many people thought that planes were the cheapest way of preventing future aggression or of winning a war if one came.

Most British politicians hoped that judicious policies of compromise, conciliation and concession would prevent conflict. Such policies were later called appeasement. The meaning of the word has been so stretched and distorted since 1939 that some historians believe the word should no longer be used. Appeasement can be used to cover almost every manifestation of British diplomacy between the two world wars. Or it can be used more specifically to describe Chamberlain's policies to Germany in 1937 and 1938. Since the Second World War appeasement has tended to have a derogatory meaning, and the word is often used to mean a craven surrender to force. But for most of the inter-war years, appeasement was seen as a positive concept: the continuation of a long British diplomatic tradition of trying to settle disputes peacefully. Those who opposed appeasement were seen as cranks or war-mongers. Only the failure of Neville Chamberlain's policies in 1938–9 (when he actually abandoned appeasement!) turned appeasement into a pejorative term.

British governments throughout the inter-war years, aware of Britain's vulnerability, did their best to avoid conflict. Their policies ultimately failed. Was that failure inevitable? Was the Treaty of Versailles to blame? Were some statesmen more responsible than others? Would the British Empire inevitabily have disintegrated? Were the years 1919–39 years of retreat and decline? Or is it better to see the period, in Medlicott's words, as 'a long process of adaptation to the realities of the modern world', rather than as a period of decline? These are questions to bear in mind as you read the rest of this book. Historians continue to debate them. There are no easy answers!

Making notes on 'Introduction: Peace-making and Policy-making'

This introductory chapter aims to provide you with a framework for understanding the making of British foreign and imperial policy after 1919. You need to be aware that historians have very different views about the strengths and weaknesses of Britain's international position. On the one hand, Britain seemed to have emerged from the First World

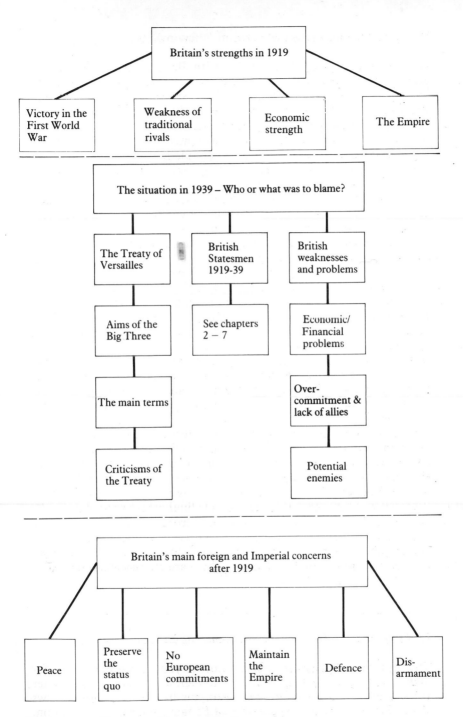

Summary – Peace-making and Policy-making

War as a first class great power. On the other, she was almost certain to face serious problems in the years ahead.

The chapter should also provide you with essential information about the aims of the 1919 peacemakers (especially Lloyd George) and the terms of the Treaty of Versailles. Understanding of the treaty is essential if you are make sense of Anglo-German relations in the inter-war period, so try to ensure that you make careful notes. You must also think carefully about the criticisms of the treaty which were made at the time and which have been made since. Try to decide whether the peacemakers (particularly Lloyd George) should be blamed or praised for their efforts.

Finally your notes should ensure that you have an awareness of the key concerns of most British governments after 1919.

Answering essay questions on 'Introduction: Peace-making and Policy-making'

Information from this chapter will help you to answer specific questions on the role of Lloyd George in the 1919 peace settlement. Such questions might include the following:

1 'Lloyd George bears the main responsibility for the – flawed – Treaty of Versailles'. To what extent would you agree or disagree with this comment?
2 Assess critically the role of Lloyd George at the Paris peace conference in 1919.

Question 2 is worth some attention. The important word is 'Assess'. At a higher level of study you will rarely be asked simply to describe what happened; invariably, the questions will be about why things happened. In many questions you will be asked to 'examine', 'analyse', 'explain' or 'assess'. In responding to such questions, it is never enough merely to write down information. To earn a good mark you must structure and shape your information to meet the exact wording of the question you are answering. A vital part of preparing to tackle an essay question based on an assessment of anything is consciously to identify the criteria you will use in making your judgement. It is best to state these explicitly in your essay. What criteria would you employ in assessing Lloyd George's role at the Paris peace conference?

Question 2 might be approached in the following way:
a) Begin with a short introductory paragraph describing the approach you intend to follow. Indicate some of the various assessments which historians have made (eg Lloyd George has been both blamed

and praised for his role in 1919). What is your verdict going to be?
b) You should then write a series of paragraphs (possibly 4 to 6), each one assessing a different aspect of the issue. Try to decide which issues you would select as paragraph points.
c) You must write a concluding paragraph. You should use this to draw together the major points you have tried to make in order to give an overall judgement. How would you assess Lloyd George's role at Versailles? Are you going to praise or blame him? Or are you going to (sensibly but perhaps not very bravely!) sit on the fence?

Source-based questions on 'Introduction: Peace-making and Policy-making'

1 The Treaty of Versailles
Read the extract from Lloyd George's Fontainbleu Memorandum on page 6, and the War Guilt clause on pages 7–9, and study the map on page 8. Answer the following questions:
a) Which one of the other two members of the 'Big Three' was most likely to agree with the sentiments expressed in the Fontainbleu Memorandum? Explain your answer. (**3 marks**)
b) To which 'small states' was Lloyd George probably referring? (**2 marks**)
c) Lloyd George seems concerned that Germany should not be 'unjustly treated'. Yet most Germans felt that the War Guilt clause was totally unjust. Why was this? (**3 marks**)
d) Why might Lloyd George have agreed to accept the War Guilt clause? (**3 marks**)
e) Does the evidence from the map suggest that Lloyd George managed to achieve most of his objectives at the Paris peace conference? Explain your answer. (**4 marks**)

2 Continuity in Britain's Foreign Policy
Read the extract from the 1926 secret Memorandum on page 16 and study the list of British governments, Prime Ministers and Foreign Secretaries in the period 1919–39 on page 16. Answer the following questions:
a) Why, according to the 1926 Memorandum, was Britain so keen on peace and how did she hope to maintain it? (**2 marks**)
b) Comment on the Memorandum's reference to the 'preservation of the status quo'. (**2 marks**)
c) What does the evidence from the list of British governments suggest about the likely consistency and continuity of British foreign policy in the period 1919–39? (**3 marks**)

d) According to the list of British governments, which four men would appear to have had most control over British foreign policy in the period 1919–39? What criteria have you used for your selection of the four men? (**4 marks**)

e) Which party was in power when the Memorandum was written? If a different party had been in power was it likely that Britain's aims in foreign policy would have been markedly different or much the same? Explain your answer. (**4 marks**)

CHAPTER 2

The Illusion of Peace 1919–31

1 The Problems of Peace-making

a) Introduction

In January 1919 the leaders of 32 countries, representing some 75 per cent of the world's population, assembled in Paris to make peace with the defeated Central Powers. Many criticisms have been made of the way the conference was conducted: the decision of the Allied leaders to participate in the work of detailed negotiation personally; the 'secret diplomacy'; the fact that representatives of Russia, Germany and the other defeated powers were excluded from the peace-making process; the fact that no agreement had been reached on the programme to be followed or how the conference was to be organised; and the domination of the small powers by the great ones. Even the choice of Paris as a venue has been questioned: wartime passions ran higher there than in almost any other possible location. (Lloyd George had originally proposed Geneva for the venue, but had deferred in the end to French wishes – a decision he later regretted.)

Criticisms of the peace-making process have sometimes been exaggerated. However, it would be difficult to exaggerate the seriousness of the problems which the peace-makers faced. They somehow had to cope with a whole series of conflicting treaty commitments, promises and pronouncements which had been made during the war. The breakdown of the German (Hohenzollern), Russian (Romanov), Austro-Hungarian (Habsburg) and Turkish (Ottoman) empires had resulted in economic chaos, famine, and outbursts of nationalism – sometimes violent – throughout central and eastern Europe and the Near East. There was the fear that Bolshevism might spread westwards from Russia and threaten the whole of Europe. The peace-makers were also aware that they could not act in isolation – the peace settlement would need to reflect the intense popular feeling within their own countries – and that decisions would have to be made quickly. Perhaps the main difficulty was that the 'Big Three' – Lloyd George, Clemenceau and Woodrow Wilson – held very different views about how to ensure a durable peace settlement.

The conclusion of a satisfactory peace treaty with Germany was the major concern of the 'Big Three'. Their aims, the terms of the Treaty of Versailles and the verdicts of both contemporaries and historians on the Treaty have been examined in chapter 1. Once the Treaty had been signed, Lloyd George and the other leading statesmen returned home. Therefore, the completion of treaties with Germany's allies was left to less eminent Allied representatives. This was done in a piecemeal fashion between July 1919 and August 1920. The treaties with Austria, Hungary, Bulgaria and Turkey were to be as controversial (both at the time and since) as the Treaty of Versailles.

b) Eastern Europe

Eastern Europe posed severe difficulties for the peace-makers. The Habsburg Empire had fallen apart. Countries such as Poland and Czechoslovakia already effectively existed. Russia, in the hands of the Bolsheviks and in the throes of a civil war, had no representatives at the peace conference, and therefore nothing involving the country could be settled.

France, Britain and America had divergent – but not completely dissimilar – aims in eastern Europe. Some British and French statesmen would have liked to retain the Habsburg Empire in some form, if only as a potential counter-weight to Russia and Germany. But given the intense nationalist feeling among the peoples of the former empire, this was impossible. France supported the creation of sizeable, economically viable and strategically defensible states, which they hoped would be strong enough to withstand either German or Russian pressure. Britain had no wish to produce a settlement that left large numbers of Germans outside Germany, but was concerned that the new states should be strong enough to resist Bolshevik pressure. On the whole, most Allied statesmen supported the American principle of self-determination and efforts were made to redraw the frontiers of eastern Europe along ethnic lines.

However, the mixture of national groups in eastern Europe meant that the establishment of frontiers was certain to cause massive problems. To make matters worse, while the peace-makers in Paris tried to redraw national boundaries, various ethnic groups in eastern Europe battled it out in a series of military confrontations. The borders that finally came into existence owed as much to the outcome of these clashes as to the negotiations at Paris.

Ultimately, in 1920, treaties were signed with Austria (the Treaty of St Germain), Hungary (the Treaty of Trianon), and Bulgaria (the Treaty of Neuilly). All the defeated powers had to pay reparations and lost large slices of territory. Austria, for example, lost land to Poland, Czechoslovakia, Italy and Yugoslavia, with the result that her population was reduced from 28 million to less than 8 million.

The eastern treaties, combined with various settlements along the Russian borderlands, ultimately created a string of new states from Finland to Yugoslavia (see the map on page 8), whose disputes over exact frontiers continued well into the 1920s. Although the peace-makers did their best to apply the principle of self-determination, all over eastern Europe large communities found themselves governed by people of a different ethnic group. Czechoslovakia, for example, had a population of about 14,500,000, made up of Czechs, Slovaks, Germans, Hungarians, Ruthenians and Poles. Yugoslavia was even more mixed. Nothing short of massive population transfers could have resolved the problem.

British politicians throughout the 1920s shared Lloyd George's view that the eastern frontiers were unsound and the new (or enlarged) states unstable and unreliable. Bulgaria, Hungary and Austria were left bitter and resentful and there were social, economic and political tensions in almost every eastern European state. The fact that many of the new states contained large minorities of discontented Germans was a further problem. It seemed likely, at some time in the future, that Germany would press for territorial modifications, especially with Poland. British governments, therefore, were reluctant to commit themselves to defend the territorial settlement in eastern Europe. The best that could be hoped for was that some peaceful means could be found to revise a flawed settlement.

c) Turkey

Britain had a greater interest in the Middle East than in Eastern Europe and in consequence took a greater part in deciding the fate of the Ottoman Empire. The Treaty of Sevres, signed in 1920, satisfied most of Britain's concerns. The Straits, linking the Black Sea and the Mediterranean, were to be de-militarised and placed under international supervision. The Arab areas of the Ottoman Empire were given (as mandates) to Britain and France. France acquired what is today Syria and Lebanon. Britain acquired present-day Israel, Jordan and Iraq. Eastern Thrace, the Gallipoli peninsula, Smyrna and several Aegean islands were given to Greece.

However, Mustafa Kemal, a Turkish nationalist and war hero, now led a national uprising and by 1920 had won the support of most Turks. Lloyd George, who had no love for the Turks, saw no reason to recognise Kemal's authority. In March 1921, Greece, with Lloyd George's tacit approval if not active encouragement, declared war on Kemal's government. Britain confined her aid to moral support, and the Greeks failed to make much headway. Kemal meanwhile came to terms with Italy, France and the USSR. In 1922 Turkish forces launched a major offensive in Asia Minor. Greek resistance quickly collapsed and it soon became apparent that the Turks might threaten the British forces occupying the international zone of the Straits. Lloyd George seemed prepared to go to war to defend the Straits, even though Britain could expect no help from France and only lukewarm support from the British Dominions. At the end of September Turkish forces reached Chanak, the British base. Military confrontation was only avoided because of the cool judgement of the British commanders on the spot. The Turks, who had no wish to go to war with Britain, agreed to respect the international zone. Some saw the Chanak crisis as an example of successful firmness in the face of aggression and thus a victory for Lloyd George. But others saw the whole affair as unnecessary war-mongering on Lloyd George's part and the Chanak crisis helped contribute to his downfall in October 1922.

In the long term, the British stand at Chanak had little effect. Negotiations with Kemal's government were skilfully handled by Lord Curzon, the Foreign Secretary, and a new agreement, the Treaty of Lausanne, was signed in 1923. This was the first significant revision of the Peace Settlement. Turkey retained Eastern Thrace, Smyrna and the Aegean islands she had won back from Greece. She no longer had to pay reparations, but she accepted the loss of her Arab territories and agreed that the Straits should remain demilitarised and open to the ships of all nations in time of peace. Britain's main interests were thus preserved. Moreover relations with Turkey now considerably improved. Britain, therefore, had good reason to be satisfied with the new settlement.

d) Italy

Italy had looked to the peace settlement to give her the considerable amounts of land which had been promised in 1915 when she had entered the war. This would compensate for her heavy losses in the war and help make her the great power she had so long yearned to be. However, the peace settlement failed to provide all the promised territory, and caused considerable resentment in Italy.

In 1922 Benito Mussolini, leader of the Italian Fascist party, seized power in Rome. He demanded revision of the peace settlement and talked of making Italy a great imperial power. He soon showed he was prepared to involve himself in dramatic foreign policy escapades. His ambitions in the Mediterranean, regarded as a vital link in Britain's world-wide communication chain, seemed to pose a direct threat to the British Empire.

Mussolini won some modest gains in Africa, succeeded in annexing the port of Fiume on the border with Yugoslavia, and strengthened Italy's hold over Albania. However, for most of the 1920s the Italian leader kept a low profile, only involving himself in adventures where some glory could be won on the cheap. Some British statesmen, such as Churchill and Lloyd George, expressed admiration for his achievements in Italy. Neither he nor Fascism, which appeared to be a uniquely Italian phenomenon, posed the serious threat in the 1920s that some had feared they would.

2 Anglo-Soviet Relations 1917–31

a) Hostility to Bolshevism

Britain's reactions to the abdication of Tsar Nicholas II in March 1917 had been generally positive. At last it seemed Russia might join the ranks of the genuine parliamentary democracies. But the coming to power of Lenin and the Bolshevik Party in November 1917 was greeted with a more mixed reaction. Many on the British left sympathised with communism and extolled the proletarian triumph. But public opinion in general seems to have been hostile, especially when Lenin made peace with Germany at the Treaty of Brest Litovsk in March 1918, thus enabling the Germans to concentrate all their forces on the Western Front. This anger was exacerbated when the Bolsheviks nationalised all foreign enterprises in Russia without compensation and made it clear that they had no intention of repaying the war debts due to Britain.

Most Conservative and Liberal MPs were implacably opposed to Lenin and agreed with Winston Churchill when he spoke of 'the foul baboonery of Bolshevism'. Churchill was all for sending British forces into Russia to destroy the Bolsheviks before they could sow the seeds of revolution elsewhere in the world, possibly even in Britain. From 1918 to 1920 British government policy was one of outright hostility to the Bolshevik regime.

In March 1918 Britain sent troops to Murmansk and Archangel to ensure that war supplies which had been sent there did not fall into Bolshevik hands. As Russia plunged into civil war, these troops began to cooperate with 'White' forces which were trying to topple Lenin and the 'Reds'. Although Churchill and other Cabinet ministers fully supported this interventionist policy, Lloyd George was more cautious, particularly after the armistice with Germany. He tended to the view that the Russians should resolve their own internal crisis. However, anxious to retain Conservative support, he did send some military help (about 30,000 troops in all) and considerable financial assistance (some £100 million) to the Whites. Although it had seemed possible for a time that the Whites might succeed, by the end of 1919 the Bolsheviks had established control in Russia (although no major power yet recognised them) and British forces were withdrawn.

b) Divided Opinions in Britain

Left-wing opinion, including the Labour Party and the TUC, had condemned British intervention in Russia, representing it as a capitalist attack on the proletariat. In 1920 Polish forces tried to take over the Ukraine from Russia. The Bolsheviks fought back and the Red Army looked as though it might capture Warsaw, the Polish capital. The British government considered sending help to Poland. The Labour movement again opposed any kind of British intervention. London dockers refused to load a ship carrying munitions already bought by the Polish government. Some 350 Councils of Action sprang up throughout Britain and even moderate Labour supporters seemed ready to support a general strike in a 'Hands off Soviet Russia' campaign. However, the Poles, with French assistance, succeeded in driving back the Soviet forces and Russia and Poland now made peace. British intervention, therefore, was no longer an issue and the domestic crisis ended.

The left-wing in Britain had considerable sympathy for the communist 'experiment' in Russia. The British Communist Party actively identified its aims with those of the Bolsheviks. Although it was very small (it had only 4000 members in 1920), many trade unionists, rank and file Labour supporters and radical intellectuals (such as H.G. Wells and George Bernard Shaw) were ready to applaud the Russian 'workers' state', especially at a time of considerable industrial unrest at home. Some even hoped for a proletarian revolution within Britain. However, Ramsay MacDonald and other leaders of the Labour Party were highly suspicious of the anti-democratic and violent nature of Bolshevism and drew a clear distinction between socialism and communism.

By 1920–1 MacDonald held not dissimilar views to Lloyd George. The Prime Minister still had little enthusiasm for Lenin. But he now believed that wooing Russia back into a commercial relationship with Europe would have far more effect in softening the Bolshevik regime than a policy of armed intervention. In a Commons debate in 1920 he went so far as to say that the moment trade was established 'Communism would go'. However, many of his Conservative supporters wished to see the USSR (as Russia was re-named in 1922) kept in diplomatic isolation and continued to remain deeply suspicious of the Bolsheviks' intentions. There was some substance to these fears. Lenin and many other Communists hoped that other European countries would follow Russia's example. The Comintern – 'the general staff of world revolution', according to Lenin – was founded in 1919 precisely to achieve this objective. The (unsuccessful) Sparticist risings in Germany, the establishment of (short-lived) Communist regimes in Hungary and Bavaria in 1919 and the (failed) attempts to impose a Communist government in Poland in 1920 lent some credibility to Lenin's hopes and British Conservatives' fears. Many Conservatives also believed that Russian agents were at work stirring up anti-British feeling in India, Afghanistan and Iran.

To a considerable extent, after 1920 Anglo-Soviet relations depended on which party was in power in Britain, with Conservative governments far less willing to do business with the USSR than Labour. However, policy also shifted in response to changes in Soviet objectives. In 1921 Russia suffered appalling famine which provoked something of a U-turn in Lenin's thinking and the adoption of the New Economic Policy, a step down from the notion of total Communism. Soviet foreign policy began to speak with two voices. The first, that of the Comintern, still preached World Revolution and claimed that Britain was the spearhead of capitalist-imperialist aggression which was aiming to destroy Communism in Russia. The second, that of the Soviet government, urged the need for normal relations with those countries – including Britain – whose economic cooperation they needed. British diplomats had difficulty adjusting to this double-speak.

c) Conciliatory Moves

However, Lloyd George pressed ahead with negotiations with the USSR, hoping that the re-establishment of trade relations would help the ailing British economy. He also feared that if Russia continued to be treated as an outcast she might well ally with the other European pariah – Germany. Such an alliance might well threaten Europe's peace and stability. In March 1921 an Anglo-Soviet trade agreement was finally signed. Under its terms each side agreed to refrain from hostile propaganda. The Soviet government recognised in principle its obligations to private citizens in Britain who had not yet been paid for goods supplied to Russia during the war. However, Britain (along with many other nations) was still unwilling to grant full recognition to Lenin's government.

In 1922 Lloyd George tried to widen the scope of the Anglo-Russian trade treaty and to bring Russia back into the mainstream European economic structure at the World Economic Conference at Geneva. The British Prime Minister had a series of secret discussions with the Soviet delegates, but made little progress. The chief stumbling-block was Russia's refusal to pay compensation for the substantial pre-war Western investment in Russia. Lloyd George's worst fears seemed to have been realised when, in the middle of the conference, Russia and Germany announced they had signed the Treaty of Rapallo. This brought substantial economic and military benefits to both Germany and Russia. Germany was able to produce and test new weapons in Russia – weapons which she was banned from producing in Germany. Russia received useful German technical expertise. However, despite this pact of 'mutual friendship', both Russia and Germany (to the relief of Britain and France) continued to regard each other with considerable suspicion.

After the fall of Lloyd George in October 1922, Lord Curzon played a more prominent role in foreign affairs. He was much less committed to economic cooperation with Russia and threatened to end the trade agreement because of the repeated Soviet violation of the undertaking to refrain from hostile propaganda. The Russian reply was conciliatory and the agreement survived. But Curzon would take no further steps towards recognising the legitimacy of the Bolshevik regime.

In 1924 the Labour Party came to power. Ramsay MacDonald, who was both Prime Minister and Foreign Secretary, immediately resumed full diplomatic relations with Russia and was soon negotiating for a new trade treaty which he hoped would provide an increased market for Britain. The main obstacle was still the question of debts to British creditors. In August an Anglo-Soviet Agreement – on both general and commercial matters – was finally reached. There were promises of friendship and the cessation of propaganda. In the event of a satisfactory arrangement over the settlement of British debts, the British government agreed to guarantee a loan of £30,000,000. The agreement, said one contemporary, was merely an agreement to agree if and when the parties could agree to agree. However, many Conservatives and Liberals, suspicious of the Labour Party's policy of rapprochement with the USSR, saw the Agreement as more important and more threatening. The Liberals withdrew their support from the minority Labour government and in the general election which followed, Labour was charged with being susceptible to Communist pressure.

A few days before polling day, the Daily Mail published a letter, purporting to be from Gregory Zinoviev, head of the Comintern. This letter urged the British Communist Party to work for the proposed Anglo-Soviet Agreement because of the opportunities for subversion which it would provide. It also issued instructions for all types of seditious activities. The Conservatives used the letter as a final 'red scare', denouncing Labour as accomplices or dupes of the Communists. The Zinoviev letter, which may or may not have been a forgery, probably made no substantial difference to the election result. Even before the letter was published, the Conservatives had succeeded in tarring the Labour Party as pandering to communism. Due largely to the collapse of the Liberal vote, the Conservatives won a resounding victory.

d) Anglo-Soviet Problems 1924–31

Not surprisingly, Anglo-Soviet relations now deteriorated. Prime Minister Baldwin did not ratify the Anglo-Soviet Agreement. A large USSR donation to the Miners' Federation during the 1926 General Strike led to angry protests by the British Cabinet. The Arcos affair caused a further rift. Arcos – the All Russian Co-operative Society – was the main organisation through which Anglo-Soviet trade was conducted. A raid on its London premises in 1927 led to Baldwin accusing the USSR of using Arcos as a means of directing 'military espionage and subversive activities throughout the British Empire and North and South America'. Britain broke off diplomatic relations and ended all trade agreements.

The Labour government which came to power in 1929 restored diplomatic contacts and signed a new commercial treaty with Russia in 1930. But it proved impossible to reach agreement over Russian debts and the possibility of British loans. No intimacy developed between the two countries. Stalin, who was now effectively in control in Russia, was primarily concerned with economic development. MacDonald's government was content to see the USSR remain on the periphery of Europe.

3 The German Question in the 1920s

a) Allied Disagreement

British foreign policy in the 1920s was dominated by the German question. In 1919 it had been generally assumed that Germany would honour the Versailles peace treaty as other defeated nations had honoured peace treaties in the past. But most Germans were determined to avoid carrying out the terms of the peace settlement. In consequence the enforcement of the Treaty of Versailles required the same determination and co-operation amongst the victorious powers as winning the war had done. The reverse occurred. By the start of the 1920s Britain and France disagreed on just about everything, while America divorced herself from events in Europe.

French leaders were particularly concerned about Germany's efforts to undo the treaty. France had a land border with an embittered Germany – a country with 50 per cent more people and four times France's heavy industry. In this situation France's response was to insist upon the most stringent enforcement of the peace terms. French governments also searched for alternative structures of security. They did all they could to seek alliance with Britain and to conclude military agreements with the states of eastern Europe, such as Poland (1921) and Czechoslovakia (1924).

British governments opposed most aspects of French policy. They regarded France's efforts to encircle Germany with disapproval and were not prepared to underwrite French security in western Europe. Moreover, many British politicians soon expressed misgivings about the Treaty of Versailles and the treatment of Germany. There was increasing unease about the one-sided application of self-determination, about Germany's exclusion from the League of Nations, and about reparations. Many influential people thought that a revision of the Treaty was urgently needed if there was to be a lasting peace in Europe. The dispute about whether the treaty of Versailles was the beginning or the end of peacemaking was central to Anglo-French relations until the 1930s.

In the early 1920s international relations were dominated by two topics – reparations and security. No less than 23 summit conferences were held between 1920 and 1922. Most followed a similar pattern. British representatives urged the French to relax the provisions of Versailles, but to little effect. French leaders feared that any treaty revision would strengthen Germany and lead to her economic and military dominance in Europe. Thus the First World War would have been in vain and there would be the spectre of a German war of revenge.

In 1920 and 1921 French troops occupied several German cities when Germany violated the reparation and disarmament clauses of the Versailles treaty. Britain opposed such action. Lloyd George and his successors, Bonar Law and Baldwin, wanted to adopt policies which would appease Germany. They also wished to reduce German reparations payments and to promote Germany's economic recovery in the belief that this would help British trade. France might have been prepared to take a more conciliatory line had Britain been ready to sign a security treaty with her. But most British politicians opposed this idea.

In 1922 Britain tried to resolve the reparations issue by proposing a cancellation of both reparations and the payments of war debts to America. This idea received little favour in America, France or even in the City in London (Britain was owed four times as much as she owed the USA and would therefore have been a net loser if the scheme had been adopted!) Reparations, therefore, continued to sour Anglo-French and Franco-German relations.

b) The Occupation of the Ruhr

By December 1922 Germany had fallen hopelessly behind in its reparation payments. Poincaré, the new anti-German French leader, decided that enough was enough. In January 1923 French and Belgian troops occupied the Ruhr, the industrial heart of Germany, with the intention of forcing Germany to meet its financial obligations. The occupation of the Ruhr stirred up intense feelings of German nationalist hostility against France. German authorities adopted a policy of passive resistance, with the result that industrial production in the Ruhr ground to a halt, the German economy collapsed, and Germany suffered hyper-inflation.

The British government disliked but did not openly condemn French policy. It adopted what one contemporary described as a policy of 'surly neutrality', trying without success to resolve the crisis. Some British officials thought the Ruhr occupation was an economic disaster for Britain. In fact just the opposite was the case. British exports soared and unemployment fell as German competition disappeared. Although Poincaré faced strong British and American financial pressure, he held out stubbornly for several months, opposing any reform of the reparations settlement, supporting a Rhineland separatist movement (which soon collapsed), and finally forcing the Germans to abandon their policy of passive resistance in the Ruhr and to pay reparations.

In April 1924 a reparations committee (known as the Dawes

'In reparations Dreamland' (A David Low cartoon)

Committee after its American chairman), proposed that payments should be reduced and phased over a longer period, thus cutting the annual and total amounts to be paid in reparations. In the meantime, Germany should receive an American loan to tide her over her immediate difficulties. MacDonald, the British Prime Minister, worked hard to secure French and German acceptance of the Dawes Plan. The replacement of Poincaré by Herriot in May 1924 helped MacDonald's cause and agreement was finally reached in August 1924. Germany agreed to meet the new reparation payments. In return, France agreed to withdraw her forces from the Ruhr within one year. Both countries kept their side of the bargain. For the next few years Germany met her reparations almost in full, thanks largely to extensive American loans. Thus began the celebrated triangular flow of money between the USA and Europe. American loans enabled Germany to pay reparations to France and Britain. The Reparation payments helped Britain and France repay their American war-debts. Most historians consider the occupation of the Ruhr as a defeat for France. She had been forced to accept a substantial revision of the reparations issue and had gained nothing in return.

c) Locarno

The Ruhr occupation convinced many French statesmen that in future they should not enforce the Treaty of Versailles single-handed. Worried by the growing strength of Germany, they looked increasingly to Britain for guarantees of security. However, both Labour and Conservative governments were opposed to binding Britain to France and were opposed to French efforts to strengthen the coercive powers of the League of Nations. Balfour thought France's obsession with security was 'intolerably foolish . . . They are so dreadfully afraid of being swallowed up by the tiger that they spend all their time poking it.' Even the pro-French Austen Chamberlain, who became Foreign Secretary in November 1924, failed to persuade his Conservative Cabinet colleagues to accept anything in the way of an Anglo-French alliance.

However, in 1925 Chamberlain took up an offer from Gustav Stresemann, the German Foreign Minister. Stresemann said he was prepared to enter into an agreement with France for a joint guarantee of their frontiers in Western Europe. Thanks largely to Chamberlain's efforts, representatives from Britain, France, Germany, Italy, Poland, Czechoslovakia and Belgium met at Locarno in Switzerland in September 1925. The terms of office of the three main participants – Chamberlain, Stresemann and Briand, the French foreign minister – largely coincided, and collectively they dominated European diplomacy for the remainder of the 1920s. They were all anxious to see an improvement in Franco-German relations. Therefore the Locarno meeting was a far cry from the grim tension of earlier international conferences.

The Locarno Pact consisted of a number of agreements. It was decided that Germany should be welcomed into the League of Nations in 1926. Germany's western frontiers with France and Belgium were accepted as final and were guaranteed by Britain and Italy. Stresemann, despite British and French pressure, would not agree to the same recognition of Germany's eastern boundaries. The most he would do was state that the frontiers should not be altered by force, but he refused to put his signature to this promise. However, he was prepared to recognise the new treaties of mutual military assistance signed between France, Poland and Czechoslovakia.

At the time, the Locarno Pact was seen as a diplomatic triumph and a great landmark. Austen Chamberlain regarded it as 'the real dividing line between the years of war and the years of peace'. It seemed that Germany had been readmitted to the community of nations and that France and Germany had been reconciled. People talked of a new spirit, the 'spirit of Locarno', and Chamberlain, Briand and Stresemann were awarded the Nobel Peace Prize for their efforts. But many historians now tend to view Locarno in a less positive light. They point out that Germany did not abandon any of her ambitions in the east and that perhaps Britain encouraged these ambitions by indicating her unwillingness to underwrite Germany's eastern frontier. Chamberlain wrote: 'No British government ever will, or ever can, risk the bones of a British grenadier . . . for the Polish Corridor'.

Britain's guarantee of the western borders is also seen as little more than an empty gesture. In 1926 the British Chiefs of Staff revealed they had no plans and few forces to give substance to the new obligations. From France's point of view Locarno was a potentially worrying agreement. It clearly represented the furthest extent Britain was prepared to go in terms of supporting the Versailles settlement – and by simply giving a general pledge against aggression in the west Britain had not gone far. Indeed the British pledge was as much a guarantee to Germany as to France: a new French move into the Ruhr was now impossible. In reality the Locarno Pact did not really denote any fundamental change in British policy. The British government had no intention of being drawn into Anglo-French military talks. Britain had given a guarantee that Chamberlain was convinced would never have to be honoured.

Moreover, Locarno did not end Germany's sense of grievance or her attempts to secure revision of the Treaty of Versailles. France retained her distrust of German intentions, so much so that in 1927 she began the construction of the Maginot Line of defences along the German border. Regular meetings between Stresemann, Briand and Chamberlain after 1926 yielded little in the way of agreement. Chamberlain, in private, grumbled over Germany's ingratitude and her demands for further revision. Stresemann grumbled that further concessions to Germany took longer than he had anticipated.

However, the Locarno Pact did improve the international atmosphere of the late 1920s. Although Stresemann was a German nationalist and determined to dismantle the Versailles settlement, he saw the advantage of collaboration with the western powers and was prepared to work with Chamberlain and Briand through the League of Nations. In the late 1920s there seemed no real prospect of major conflict. In 1928 all the major powers signed the Kellogg-Briand Pact, outlawing war. In 1929 the Young Plan extended the period of reparations payments by 60 years, thus further easing the burden on Germany. As part of this package, Britain and France agreed to end their occupation of the Rhineland five years ahead of schedule. In May 1930 Briand proposed that the European nations should establish a federal link, primarily economic in character. However, the onset of the Great Depression in the 1930s ended both the Young Plan and any immediate hopes of European federalism.

4 The League of Nations

One result of the Treaty of Versailles was the creation of the League of Nations. This had its headquarters in Geneva. The Assembly of the League, composed of representatives of all the member states, met yearly and each state had one vote. Britain, France, Italy and Japan had permanent seats on the Council of the League. The Assembly could then elect 4 (later 6) further members of the Council. The Council made most of the League's decisions. By the Covenant of the League, member states agreed to a number of (somewhat vague) Articles. Perhaps the most important was Article 16 which stated that if any member of the League resorted to war, the other states should impose economic sanctions and, if necessary, take appropriate military action.

Although the League of Nations owed its inception largely to Woodrow Wilson, it soon evoked enthusiastic support in Britain, especially from the Left. British public opinion came to accept that the League was an institution with a ready-made machinery for solving all international problems peacefully. Many believed that no aggressor would dare to risk war with the 50 or so League states and that in consequence force would not be needed to uphold the principles of the League. British Foreign Ministers faithfully attended the meetings of the Assembly and the Council, aware that support for the League often brought popularity at home. The League of Nations Union soon proved to be a effective pressure group. Its chairman claimed in 1928 that 'All parties are pledged to the League . . . all Prime Ministers and ex-Prime Ministers support it . . .'

But while they might support the League in principle, few Conservative politicians really believed in its efficacy as an instrument for solving international disputes. They realised that the League's mere existence did not automatically prevent aggression and that without the USA and the USSR it was hardly a truly world-wide organisation. Military leaders pointed out that the League had no armed forces of its own and warned that it created a misleading and dangerous sense of security. In reality it depended on Britain and France resisting those countries bent on aggression. But given the League's popularity, few politicians were prepared to express these criticisms openly.

From the start, the French had hoped to fashion the League into a force to preserve the Versailles boundaries. They continued to try to strengthen the League's obligations and to make them more binding on member states. On the other hand, most British politicians favoured a looser, less binding arrangement and thought the League should function as an instrument for the peaceful adjustment of international boundaries and other disputed matters, not as a force committed to oppose all change.

In 1923 the Assembly of the League accepted a draft treaty of Mutual Assistance designed to outlaw 'aggressive war'. This proposal was strongly opposed by both the British Admiralty and the British Dominion governments. In April 1924 the Labour Prime Minister Ramsay MacDonald, who earlier had proclaimed the determination of his party to strengthen the League, decided not to support the draft treaty. Instead, in conjunction with the French Premier, Herriot, he suggested a new scheme, the Geneva Protocol. Any state refusing to submit a dispute to arbitration or rejecting the decision of an arbitrator would be regarded as an aggressor and liable to economic sanctions or even military force. There was strong British opposition to the Protocol's vague but potentially unlimited commitments and it was rejected by a new Conservative government in 1925.

The League did have some successes in the 1920s. In general it established itself as an international organisation capable of resolving disputes between minor powers and promoting a wide range of humanitarian and economic activities. It was a useful talking shop and its meetings provided good opportunities for foreign statesmen to meet and discuss outside the formal sessions. The League's status seemed to be further enhanced when Germany joined in 1926.

However, the League had little real influence. The important questions of the day were settled in the hotel rooms of the Foreign Ministers of Britain, France, Italy and (after 1926) Germany, and the small states were helpless in the face of the reality of great power politics.

5 Disarmament

In 1919 the Allies had disarmed Germany, a move seen by some as the first step in the process of general world disarmament. Members of the League of Nations agreed to disarm to 'the lowest point consistent with national safety'. Most British governments in the 1920s favoured disarmament for political and economic reasons. Defence spending was cut back. By 1932 Britain was spending only £102 million on defence, compared with £760 million in 1919–20. The army reverted to its pre-war role of imperial police force and, although the RAF preserved its separate identity, it remained small in numbers. But the most interesting developments surrounded the Senior Service – the navy.

a) Naval

Although the war had brought about the destruction of the German fleet, in 1919 there seemed every prospect of there being a naval race betwen the USA and Britain. The Admiralty was furious that the American naval building programme aimed to create a fleet larger than the Royal Navy. There was also the problem of a growing Japanese fleet in the Pacific. America was more suspicious of Japan's intentions than Britain and was anxious to end the Anglo-Japanese treaty of 1902. In November 1921 representatives of the main naval powers – the USA, Britain, France, Italy and Japan – met in Washington. This conference led to the conclusion of the 1922 Washington Naval Agreement under which capital ships allowed to the countries concerned would be in the following ratios: USA 5; Britain 5; Japan 3; Italy 1.75; and France 1.75. No new capital ships were to be constructed for ten years. Britain also agreed not to renew her alliance with Japan. It was replaced by a Four Power Treaty signed by Britain, the USA, France and Japan, guaranteeing the status quo in the Far East.

There was considerable opposition in some quarters to the Washington Treaty. Britain no longer had naval superiority. The size of her fleet would now be determined by the treaty, not by an assessment of Britain's strategic needs. The halt in capital ship building would leave Britain with an obsolescent fleet by the time construction was allowed again. British interests in the Far East would no longer be protected by the Japanese alliance. Some historians still argue that the Washington Treaty was a major catastrophe for Britain.

However, Britain did gain some advantages from the treaty. In particular she avoided a wasteful and unnecessary naval race with the USA, the cost of which would have been enormous and which America almost certainly would have won. Although Britain had sacrificed her old relationship with Japan and had thus weakened her position in the Far East, she had at least remained on good terms with the USA – and at the end of the day this was more important than remaining on good terms with Japan. For many politicians at the time, and historians since, the Washington naval disarmament system seemed to be a constructive and forward-looking act. In 1927 an attempt to limit the number of cruisers broke down, but in 1930 the USA, Britain and Japan did agree to limit their cruisers in a fixed ratio (10:10:7) and to prolong the moritorium on the building of capital ships for a further five years.

b) Military

Securing agreement about land armaments proved far more difficult. The main problem was the relationship between France and Germany. French leaders, aware that Germany was not even complying with the disarmament terms of the Treaty of Versailles, realised it would be national and political suicide to reduce her own large forces without water-tight guarantees of security. Germany, on the other hand, demanded to be treated as an equal. A Preparatory Commission on Disarmament, set up in 1926, failed to make headway because of mutual suspicion. German demands for equality were incompatible with French demands for security.

In 1928 Britain, like most powers (including Russia), endorsed the Kellogg-Briand Pact and renounced war as a means of settling international disputes. This seemed to auger well for disarmament and the maintenance of world peace.

6 Conclusion

In 1929 Viscount D'Abernon, British Ambassador to Germany in the mid-1920s, wrote that the lesson of the post-war years was not:

1 ... negative ... but positive. It is not a recital of unfortunate events which led up to a great catastrophe. It is the narrative rather of a historical period in which immense progress has been made towards pacification, and during which the international 5 suspicion diminished, and the cause of co-operation between nations appreciably advanced.

At the start of the 1930s there seemed good reason for optimism. Although many outstanding questions still menaced Franco-German relations, both countries seemed ready to settle disputes by negotiation rather than by force. Mussolini's oratory was occasionally war-like, but his escapades were minor. Bolshevik Russia had turned out to be an embarrassment rather than a serious problem. No great power in the 1920s had threatened the security of Britain or her Empire. In consequence, Britain, like many countries, had been able to run down its armed forces. Almost all the major powers had agreed to renounce war and the League of Nations seemed an effective organisation that would ensure peace.

Winston Churchill, writing in 1948, summed up the 1920s in generally encouraging terms:

1 Although old antagonisms were but sleeping, and the drumbeat of new levies was already heard, we were justified in hoping that the ground thus solidly gained would open the road to a further forward march.
5   At the end of the second Baldwin Administration [1929] the state of Europe was tranquil, as it had not been for 20 years, and was not to be for at least another 20. A friendly feeling existed towards Germany following upon our Treaty of Locarno, and the evacuation of the Rhineland by the French Army and Allied
10 contingents at a much earlier date than had been prescribed at Versailles. The new Germany took her place in the truncated League of Nations. Under the genial influence of American and British loans Germany was reviving rapidly . . . France and her system of alliances also seemed secure in Europe. The disarma-
15 ment clauses of the Treaty of Versailles were not openly violated. The German Navy was non-existent. The German Air Force was prohibited and still unborn. There were many influences in Germany strongly opposed, if only on the grounds of prudence, to the idea of war, and the German High Command could not
20 believe that the Allies would allow them to rearm.

Sally Marks, an historian, writing in 1976, had a different view.

1 A few men knew that the spirit of Locarno was a fragile foundation on which to build a lasting peace. After all, the real spirit at Locarno, behind the facade of public fellowship, was one of bitter confrontation between a fearful France flanked by the
5 unhappy east Europeans, trying to hide their humiliation and panic, and a resentful, revisionist Germany demanding even more alterations in the power balance to her benefit. Since Germany was potentially the strongest power on the continent, the private fears of her neighbours could only deepen.
10   Yet the public faces remained serene and smiling, and the ordinary European did not know about the clashes behind closed doors . . . The public facade of the Locarno conference and the treaties themselves had created an illusion of peace, and ordinary men rejoiced. Misled by a false front, Europe thankfully entered
15 upon the Locarno years, thinking that real peace had arrived at last. Of all the interwar years these were perhaps the best years, but none the less they were years of illusion.

Just as contemporaries saw good reason for optimism, so historians, like Marks, have seen good reason for pessimism. By 1931 Germany had secured substantial revision of the Treaty of Versailles. But most Germans were still not satisfied with Stresemann's achievements. Future German governments, of whatever political complexion, were likely to seek further revision, especially in eastern Europe. The power balance was clearly shifting in Germany's favour and the success of the Nazis in the 1930 German election did not auger well for the future.

There were also problems elsewhere. The situation in China was worrying. None of the various competing governments could long maintain much effective control. China's weakness was a constant temptation to Japan, which needed new markets and raw materials and which still had imperial ambitions.

Many historians have criticised the British statesmen of the 1920s for their complacency and lack of foresight. Some condemn them for not supporting French efforts to maintain the Versailles treaty. Others argue that if Britain had given France the assurances of support which she sought, French policy to Germany might not have been so intransigent. Others claim that Britain should have offered more concessions to meet some of Germany's more reasonable complaints in the hope of consolidating the German 'moderates' in power.

However, it is possible to defend British policy. Even with the benefit of hindsight, historians cannot agree whether a consistent 'hard' or 'soft' approach to Germany would have been the more effective. In the circumstances British efforts to find a 'middle way' made – and indeed still make – sense. British statesmen appreciated French security fears, but did their best to appease Germany whenever possible. After the experience of the First World War it was only natural that Britain was determined to avoid entanglements, especially military obligations, on the Continent. Nor is it certain that these, if they had existed, would have had much effect. Perhaps British policy fell between two stools, but the policy-makers did not have a crystal ball. Very few people in the 1920s – not even Winston Churchill! – foresaw the dark days ahead. Neither Germany, Italy nor Japan seemed to pose a particularly serious threat to world peace in 1930–1. Britain's relations with all three countries had been reasonably amicable throughout the 1920s. It is hard to see, even now, what rational actions the politicians of the 1920s could have taken which would have prevented the threat of Hitler, Mussolini and the Japanese militarists in the 1930s. The great world-wide depression of the 1930s, which followed in the wake of the 1929 Wall Street Crash in America, came out of the blue. Few had predicted it. Fewer still could foresee its political repercussions and the effect they would have on British foreign policy and on Britain's role in the world.

BRITISH PMs		BRITAIN AND GERMANY	BRITAIN AND THE USSR	OTHER MAJOR EVENTS
	1919			
Lloyd George (Conservative + Liberal Coalition)	1920	The Treaty of Versailles	Britain sends help to the "Whites" Russo – Polish War	Treaties with Austria, Hungary Bulgaria & Turkey
	1921	Reparations	Anglo – Russian trade agreement	
	1922			Washington Naval Conference
Bonar Law (Con)				Mussolini to power Chanak crisis
	1923	French occupation of the Ruhr		
Baldwin (Con)	1924			Efforts to strengthen the League of Nations
MacDonald (Lab)		The Dawes Plan	Britain recognizes USSR Zinoviev letter	
Baldwin (Con)	1925			
		Locarno		
	1926	Germany joins the League of Nations		
	1927		Arcos affair Break in diplomatic relations	
	1928			Kellogg – Briand Pact
	1929			
		The Young Plan	Anglo – USSR relations restored	
MacDonald (Lab)	1930			
	1931			

Summary – The Illusion of Peace

Making notes on 'The Illusion of Peace 1919–31'

This chapter is designed to show what problems British statesmen faced in this period, especially with regard to Russia and Germany, and how they attempted to tackle them. The 'German Question' was a major concern. You will need to make careful notes about why Germany was a problem and what the British government's policy to Germany was from 1919 to 1931. Historians have varying views about the wisdom and success of British policy and British statesmen in this period. You need to decide whether British policy was sensible or short-sighted.

Britain's relations with Germany tended to be much the same whichever party was in power. This was not true of Anglo-Soviet relations. Labour governments were far more sympathetic to the USSR than Conservative governments. The Conservatives were in power for most of the 1920s with the result that Anglo-Soviet relations were generally cool. Your notes should give you an understanding of the attitudes which determined the shape of British policy, as well as the main events. Bear in mind that Anglo-Russian relations, especially in the early 1920s, had considerable significance in domestic politics in Britain.

Answering essay questions on 'The Illusion of Peace 1919–31'

It is likely you will use information from this chapter to answer questions on British attitudes and policy to both Germany and Russia.

Consider the following questions on Anglo-Soviet relations:

1 Assess the policies of successive British governments towards the Soviet Union in the period 1917–31.
2 Examine and explain the changes in Britain's relationship with the Communist (Bolshevik) regimes in Russia from 1917 to 1931.
3 Account for the changing attitudes of British governments towards the Soviet Union from 1917 to 1931.
4 How far did 'a fear of Bolshevism' influence British foreign policy in the years 1917–31?

Re-arrange the questions in order of difficulty. Which do you think is the easiest and which the most difficult? Be prepared to explain why.

Many people will have identified question 2 as the easiest – probably because, on the surface, it can be answered in a straightforward, descriptive manner. It is because such questions can be answered simply – at a low level – that they are dangerous. It is very easy to know a lot about the subject, to write a long, narrative, year-by-year answer, but to score only half marks. Many students simply describe the events, and forget to explain them. Why did British governments adopt the policies to the USSR that they did? In what ways did the policies of Conservative and Labour governments differ and why? How did developments and events in the USSR effect British policy?

Question 4 is probably the most difficult. This is because it deals with the whole of British foreign policy, not just Anglo-Soviet relations. Many students rush into this type of question and write everything they know about Anglo-Soviet relations. 'Fear of Bolshevism' certainly influenced different British statesmen at different times. But what other factors influenced British foreign policy in the period 1919 to 1931? To what extent did 'fear of Bolshevism' even determine Anglo-Russian relations? It is worth drawing up a rough plan for question 4. If you can tackle the hard questions with confidence then you have even less to fear from the easier ones!

Source-based questions on 'The Illusion of Peace 1919–31'

1 Reparations
Examine the cartoon reproduced on page 33. Answer the following questions:
a) Why in the cartoon are:
    i) loans shown as balloons
    ii) the financial experts shown as sinister figures? (**4 marks**)
b) When do you think the cartoon first appeared? Give reasons for your answer. (**5 marks**)
c) Why should a British cartoonist be sympathetic to Germany? (**6 marks**)

2 The Situation at the End of the 1920s
Read the accounts of Viscount D'Abernon, Winston Churchill and Sally Marks on pages 39 and 40. Answer the following questions:
a) Why was Viscount D'Abernon optimistic about the future in 1929? (**2 marks**)
b) Comment on the terms 'the spirit of Locarno' and the 'Locarno years' in the extract written by Sally Marks. (**3 marks**)
c) Why does Sally Marks refer to the Locarno years as 'years of illusion'? (**3 marks**)
d) In what ways – if any – does Winston Churchill's account support the view of the Viscount D'Abernon? (**3 marks**)
e) In what ways – if any – does Winston Churchill's account support the view of Sally Marks? (**3 marks**)
f) Comment on the different perspectives of D'Abernon, Winston Churchill and Sally Marks. (**6 marks**)

CHAPTER 3

The Empire 1919–39

1 Introduction

a) The British Empire in 1919

At the end of the First World War the British Empire seemed to be at its peak. In November 1918 Lord Curzon, then Lord President of the Council but soon to beome Foreign Secretary, told the House of Lords, 'The British flag has never flown over a more powerful and united empire . . . Never did our voice count more in the councils of nations; or in the determining of the future destinies of mankind.' The peace settlements with Germany and Turkey resulted in Britain acquiring a wide variety of new territories and new peoples. The fact that these territories were to be ruled as mandates under the League of Nations seemed to make little difference. What mattered was that one quarter of the world's land surface was part of the British Empire. Moreover, unlike before 1914, Britain seemed to face no competition for empire. Germany was shattered by defeat; France had suffered grievous casualties and was an ally (of sorts); Bolshevik Russia had been weakened by revolution and civil war; and the USA seemed anxious to retreat into isolationism.

Nor was Britain's influence confined to the 'formal' empire of territorial possessions and protectorates. Britain had long been able to exert her will over regions by means other than direct colonial rule. After 1918 she effectively controlled a large number of strategically important states in the Middle East. She also had financial and commercial pre-eminence in many areas, such as Argentina. Britain regarded her position and influence in these 'client' states as of no less importance than her authority in her colonial territories. No other colonial power aspired to – or enjoyed – the same degree of global influence.

Ultimately British control rested upon her ability to keep order in her 'formal' empire and in her ability to persuade or frighten 'client' states into cooperation. The British (and Indian) army proved itself an effective force in several small-scale imperial campaigns after 1918, as in Egypt in 1919. The British navy, although challenged by the fleets of the USA and Japan, remained strong. Britain could also use the RAF. Some MPs disliked the idea of indiscriminate aerial bombing of rebel villages but 'air control', which was cheap and effective, was supported by both Labour and Conservative governments. Winston Churchill, among others, was quite prepared to use poison gas against troublesome natives.

Most British people were still proud of their Empire. Few questioned

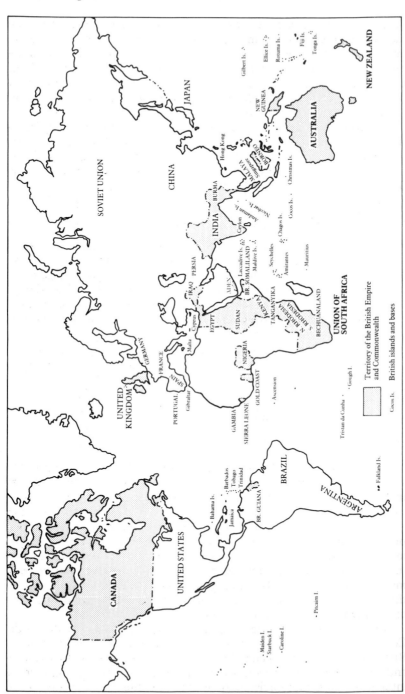

SOVIET UNION

JAPAN

CHINA

UNITED KINGDOM

GERMANY

FRANCE

SPAIN

PORTUGAL

Gibraltar

Malta

Cyprus

EGYPT

IRAQ

PERSIA

ADEN

BR. SOMALILAND

SUDAN

NIGERIA

GAMBIA

SIERRA LEONE

GOLD COAST

Ascension

KENYA

TANGANYIKA

N. RHODESIA

S. RHODESIA

BECHUANALAND

UNION OF SOUTH AFRICA

Tristan da Cunha

Gough I.

Cocos Is.

INDIA

BURMA

Hong Kong

Ceylon

Andaman Is.

Nicobar Is.

Laccadive Is.

Maldive Is.

Chagos Is.

Cocos Is.

Christmas Is.

Seychelles

Amirantes

Mauritius

MALAYA

SARAWAK

BORNEO

Singapore

NEW GUINEA

AUSTRALIA

NEW ZEALAND

Gilbert Is.

Ellice Is.

Rotuma Is.

Fiji Is.

Tonga Is.

CANADA

UNITED STATES

Bahama Is.

Barbados

Tobago

Trinidad

Jamaica

BR. GUIANA

BRAZIL

ARGENTINA

Falkland Is.

Maiden I.

Starbuck I.

Caroline I.

Pitcairn I.

Territory of the British Empire and Commonwealth

British islands and bases

The British Empire after the First World War

the moral and technical superiority of Britain's civilisation. Most saw the Empire as an efficient and benevolent system which brought peace, prosperity and happiness to less fortunate areas until such time as the peoples of those areas could safely manage their own affairs. Most British politicians assumed it would take decades, perhaps even centuries, before most of the peoples in Britain's African and Asian territories were ready for independence.

However, by 1919, some countries within the Empire had acquired a large degree of independence. These countries – Canada, Australia, New Zealand and South Africa – were known as Dominions. Some people in the Dominions preferred to see themselves as part of the British 'Commonwealth' rather than part of the British Empire.

b) The Importance of the Empire 1919–39

For most politicians, the preservation of the Empire remained a priority. All governments – Liberal, Labour and Conservative – saw the Empire as a considerable – or potentially considerable – economic asset. Before 1914 Britain had always traded more with the outside world than with her formal possessions; but in the inter-war years, the Empire was increasingly important to Britain's trading position, as the statistics show.

	Percentage of British Imports from the Empire	Percentage of British Exports to the Empire
1910–14	25	36
1920–4	27	37
1925–9	28	42
1930–4	31	42
1935–9	39.5	49

Throughout the 1920s many Conservative MPs hoped to introduce some kind of imperial tariff protection which would obstruct foreign imports, encourage inter-imperial trade and make the Empire economically self-sufficient and less vulnerable to foreign competition. In 1926 an Empire Marketing Board was set up to 'bring the Empire alive' and promote the sale of British and Empire goods. In 1932 Britain finally introduced imperial protection – with mixed results. British manufacturers certainly gained some benefit, but their dependence on imperial markets perhaps made British industry less competitive in the rest of the world. Britain possibly paid more than she needed to for food and other raw materials from the Empire.

Some Conservatives, such as Leo Amery, Secretary of State for the Colonies from 1924–9, saw imperialism not only as a solution to Britain's economic problems, but also as a useful antidote to socialism and a way of winning the support of the working class. Throughout the inter-war years imperialist supporters, like the 'press baron' Lord

Beaverbrook, tried to sell the idea of Empire to the British people. Many imperialist groups, such as the Royal Empire Society and the British Empire Union, were established. Attempts were made to include some explanation of the Empire in schools where there were Empire songs and Empire essay-writing competitions. BBC radio also played an important role in promoting the Empire. Empire Day (24 May – Queen Victoria's birthday), for example, was given great prominence on the radio in the 1920s and 30s. The King's Christmas Day broadcasts (from 1932) also had a strong imperial flavour. In 1932 the BBC actually began an Empire Service which broadcast to all the countries of the Empire. Lord Reith, head of the BBC, saw radio as a force which might help to unite the Empire and the BBC usually portrayed the Empire as a 'good thing'.

The martial virtues of imperial heroes were popularised by children's authors and by many successful adult thriller and adventure writers. The courage of the men who defended the Empire was a theme that was also exploited by both British and American film-makers. Many popular feature films (such as *The Drum* and *The Four Feathers*) gave a very positive image of the British imperial system and were very influential in forming people's attitudes to the Empire. A portrayal of the adventurous and exotic aspects of the Empire was recognised by the armed services as a useful way to attract recruits.

c) Imperial Weaknesses

However, although the British Empire might have seemed impressive to outsiders and to many within, in reality it was far from the political union that the expression the 'British Empire' implied. The British government did not rule over an ordered phalanx of colonial governments. The Dominions were more or less self-governing. The status of the 80 other territories in the Empire varied enormously. Most of these colonies or dependencies had a governor who had a small council to advise him on day-to-day policy and a larger assembly to give legal validity to laws and taxes. But there was no logic and little system in the Empire's constitutional, political or economic structure. Nor was there a single departmental voice on imperial affairs. The Foreign Office supervised Britain's relations with the client states and semi-colonies. The Dominion Office dealt with the Dominions. The Indian Viceroy was supervised by the India Office. The rest were overseen by the Colonial Office.

Whatever the dreams of imperial enthusiasts, in reality the British Empire did not match up. It was a hotch-potch collection of states and territories at different stages of political development, with little in common save the connection with Britain. This was often tenuous. Wherever possible Britain relied on indirect – and cheap – methods of control. This meant that tribal leaders, royal families or influential 'cliques' often retained considerable power in the colonies. There was limited central interference. Even determined Colonial Secretaries were unable to make progress against the pressures of so many different interests, coupled with lack of government money and public indifference. Grandiose schemes for an imperial economic system never matured. Little was done which was bold or imaginative. To make matters worse even committed imperialists, such as Leo Amery and Winston Churchill, could not agree on exactly which path imperialism should follow. Both men were Conservatives; but Amery favoured a loosely controlled 'commonwealth', in which the dominions would have considerable freedom to control their own destinies; whereas Churchill thought that Britain should keep and exert far more central control.

After 1918 the empire was to be subject to various strains, both internal and external, which threatened its existence. Perhaps the spread of nationalism was the most direct threat. Most dominions sought to assert their autonomy and independence from Britain. In Africa and Asia new educated elites increasingly resented British rule. The growing force of nationalism was reflected in episodes such as the disturbances in India in 1919–20, and the anti-British riots in Egypt in 1919.

Many British people, raised to believe in the virtues of parliamentary democracy, found it increasingly difficult to reconcile this with the paternalistic idea of Empire. There were increasing doubts, especially on the left, about the justice of Britain's imperial rule, particularly when violence had to be used against nationalist opposition. Many Labour MPs were anti-imperialist or at best suspicious of imperialist motives. There was increasing concern about the rights of native peoples. Many Britons were not convinced that expenditure on imperial defence (rather than welfare) was in Britain's best interest or in the interests of the colonial peoples.

The sheer cost of administering and defending such a heterogeneous collection of territories was a major problem. The growth of Empire in the nineteenth century had been fuelled by commercial and industrial growth at home. But from the 1870s Britain's share of the world's trade had been declining. Britain's old industries – textiles, iron and steel, and engineering – became less competitive and new industries were slow to develop. To make matters worse, many of Britain's overseas investments, on which she had depended to balance the books, had been sold to pay for the First World War. In the 1930s Britain's balance of payments began to go seriously into the red for the first time for over 100 years. British financial resources, devastated by the costs of war and the ravages of the Depression, could not sustain large forces all over the globe. Governments reduced imperial garrisons wherever possible.

With the exception of the Indian army, the local military units in the colonies were of modest strength and could not be relied upon to suppress a local insurrection if left unsupported by British troops. In consequence the British army, soon under 200,000 strong, was posted round the world in penny packets. London had to hope that major internal security problems requiring a substantial military presence did not break out simultaneously nor coincide with an international crisis. In the early 1920s British forces were stretched near to breaking-point as they struggled to keep control in Ireland, Egypt, Iraq and India. The ambitions of Germany, Italy and Japan were to be an even more serious threat in the 1930s. British officials realised that diplomatic capitulation or military defeat would have far-reaching consequences and undermine, perhaps fatally, the prestige and authority of British rule in every colony.

Ireland, Britain's oldest and nearest 'colony' can be seen as a good example of the problems of Empire. From the 1860s Irish nationalists had been vociferously demanding Home Rule. In 1916 they rose in rebellion in Dublin. The 'Easter rising' was quickly defeated, but troubles continued and Sinn Fein, an extreme Irish nationalist party, increased its strength and support. After success in the 1918 general election, Sinn Fein MPs set up an Irish Parliament in Dublin and declared independence from Britain. The Irish Republican Army (IRA) waged a guerrilla war against British rule. The British government used the 'Black and Tans' and the 'Auxis' (Auxiliary Division) to fight the IRA. These men had a taste for fighting and were quite prepared to use terror against the terrorists. By 1921, British security forces were gaining the upper-hand over the IRA, but many British people had lost confidence in the justice of their cause. Lloyd George and Irish leaders finally agreed that the new Irish Free State should be granted 'home rule', although it would remain as a dominion within the British empire. (Britain continued to have responsibility for Ulster which was not included in the Irish Free State.)

d) Different Interpretations

Many British politicians feared that a substantial devolution of power in Ireland might lead to general imperial collapse. Many historians since have regarded the establishment of the Irish Free State as symptomatic of a gradual, grudging imperial retreat which they think characterised the inter-war years. Some believe Britain's long imperial career was already played out by 1939. They think the British people, if not their governments, lacked the resolution and conviction to hold down the growing resistance to imperial rule. They see the writing on the wall in India and elsewhere. They see changes in the more developed colonies steadily and irresistably squeezing out British influence. They claim that many British politicians were merely deluding themselves in believing that by shrewd tactics, artful concessions and ingenious constitutional rearrangements they could prolong their Empire indefinitely. These historians view the Second World War as the last straw that broke the back of the imperial camel.

But other historians have a different view. They are convinced that the British Empire was not in irreversible decline, or even in retreat, by 1939. They stress that few people in 1939 predicted the rapid decline of Empire which followed 1945. Despite the chronic economic difficulties that set in after 1920, there was no question of Britain being incapable of sustaining her imperial commitments. Indeed the economic situation, in particular Britain's dependence on imported food and need for export markets, seemed an excellent reason for the maintenance of the Empire. There was still enthusiasm in Britain for colonial rule. Most politicians represented the Empire as a vital national interest from which all groups gained. Britain still had superior military technology over non-European societies. Afro-Asian nationalism was feeble. Before 1939 it seemed to many that European control would continue indefinitely. For all its imperfections, the British imperial system still seemed a necessary part of any stable world order. It is possible to argue, therefore, that prior to 1939 the evolution of the British imperial system seemed set in a path very different from that which it was ultimately to follow. Those historians who do so are convinced that the pattern of decolonisation after 1945 was very much effected by the course and impact of the Second World War.

2 The Dominions

a) The Situation in 1919

By 1919 the Dominions – Canada, Australia, New Zealand, South Africa (and the Irish Free State after 1922) – had considerable independence. All had their own Parliaments. All, with the exception of South Africa, had large majorities of whites, most of whom were of British descent, although there were many French-speaking Canadians. In South Africa a white minority, divided between the Boers (who were of Dutch descent) and the settlers of British descent, ruled a large black majority.

By 1919 the Dominions enjoyed more or less complete internal self-government. However, Britain still controlled their foreign policies, and the decision to commit the Dominions to war in 1914 had been taken by the British Cabinet alone. The sacrifices made by the Dominions in the war strengthened the emotional links with Britain. But they also ensured that the Dominions demanded a greater say in the conduct of the war. They began to see themselves as equal partners with Britain. At the end of the war the Dominions were represented separately at both the Paris peace conference and at the League of Nations where they soon proved that they were no mere lackeys of London.

In general Britain and the Dominions had co-operated well during the war. In 1917 Lloyd George had established an Imperial War Cabinet and Dominion leaders had met in Conference in London.

Many assumed that diplomatic co-operation would continue after 1918. The Imperial War Cabinet agreed that in future British prime ministers would work out an imperial foreign policy towards the rest of the world by a process of 'continuous consultation' with the Dominion leaders. The hope that the Commonwealth might speak and act with a united voice in world affairs never died in the inter-war years. However, it proved difficult to realise.

b) Disunity

The main problem was the fact that the Dominions had separate and divergent national interests. Discussions on the renewal of the Anglo-Japanese treaty in 1920–1 showed it was difficult to please everyone – Australia and New Zealand favoured renewal; Canada opposed it. It also soon became clear that it was difficult to consult the Dominions on every issue. Britain was involved in many parts of the world and was not prepared to accept the limits on her freedom of action that 'continuous consultation' would have involved. In fact the Dominions showed no sign of being worried if Britain pursued her own policy in some areas without consulting them. But the 1922 Chanak crisis (see pages 25–6) showed that Britain could not expect automatic support from the Dominions. Britain had allowed the crisis to develop without consultation with the Dominions, and when Lloyd George appealed to the dominions to send troops to Turkey he met with varied responses. Although New Zealand offered ready support, Australia was less enthusiastic and Canada flatly refused. The South African government prudently said nothing.

In the event, no military assistance was needed, but the Chanak crisis proved that the diplomatic unity of the British Commonwealth was a fiction. The policy of 'continuous consultation' was allowed to drop. Britain pursued her own policy, and some Dominions were soon pursuing theirs. In 1923, for example, Canada signed a fishing agreement with the USA without reference to Britain. Canada also led the way in establishing its own diplomatic missions abroad.

However, there was some effort at maintaining the pretence of Commonwealth unity. Imperial Conferences, attended by the prime ministers of all the Dominions, were held in London – but at increasingly irregular intervals: 1921, 1923, 1926, 1930 and 1937. There was a Committee of Imperial Defence but it rarely had any Dominion representatives at its meetings. The Dominions spent very little on defence, had little interest in European affairs and no wish to be sucked into another European war. In the 1930s most Dominion leaders favoured appeasement. Only Australia and New Zealand made it reasonably clear that they would support Britain in almost any circumstances, while Southern Ireland was unlikely to support Britain in any situation.

c) The Balfour Declaration and the Statute of Westminster

Although the Dominions were, for most practical purposes, sovereign and independent countries, that independence was established by custom rather than by formal definition. In the 1920s there was considerable pressure from South Africa, Ireland and Canada to define dominion status more precisely. The 1926 Commonwealth Conference finally agreed on the Balfour Declaration which said that the Dominions were:

1 Autonomous communities within the British Empire, equal in
  status, in no way subordinate one to another in any aspect of their
  domestic or external affairs, though united by a common allegiance to the Crown, and freely associated as members of the
5 British Commonwealth of Nations.

Leo Amery, Secretary of State for both the Colonies and the Dominions, favoured the idea of 'equal status' and 'free association'. He thought this was the only way of preventing dissension and maintaining some unity among commonwealth countries. In his diary he recorded his thoughts about the process by which the Balfour Report came about:

1 17 November 1926
  Cabinet in the morning ... The Balfour Report threatened to
  make some trouble and after a desultory conversation it was
  decided to have an extra Cabinet in the evening ... at which the
5 old centralised view of opposition to equal status and Dominion
  autonomy was defended by Cave who is a tremendous old Tory,
  as well as by Winston (Churchill) who is really a jingo of the late
  19th century and has no sympathy with the idea of Imperial unity
  by free cooperation. Balfour and I waxed eloquent at some length
10 in the defence of the modern conception of Empire ...

  22 November 1926
  My 53rd birthday and encouraged by the almost unanimous
  chorus of approval given to the Balfour Report in every quarter. I
  think I can look on the passage of that report as the completion of
15 at any rate one of the big things I have worked for most of my life.
  But only the completion of a stage, and a stage which if neglected
  means dissolution. It all makes the need for an Imperial economic
  policy more urgent than ever ...

The Statute of Westminster in 1931 put the finishing touches to the process by which an Empire based on central authority was transferred into a Commonwealth of independent states. The Dominions now had the right to change their own constitutions and even withdraw from the Commonwealth if they so wished. Common allegiance to the Crown was now the only formal link between the Dominions and Britain.

d) Imperial Preference

The Statute of Westminster was passed at a time when constitutional questions were a long way from being uppermost in the minds of most Dominion politicians. The world-wide depression was the main concern. For many years some Conservative MPs had claimed that a self-contained Imperial Common Market would solve Britain's many economic problems. Arguments for imperial protection, however, never carried total conviction because Britain conducted most of her trade with countries which were not part of the Empire. The 1930s depression forced changes. In 1932 Britain officially abandoned free trade and introduced the Import Duties Act which imposed a 10 per cent tariff on most imports. In the same year an Imperial Economic Conference at Ottawa accepted the principle of imperial preference. The Conference resulted in a series of agreements over details of preferential trade between Britain and the Dominions and between the Dominions themselves. This did not fulfil the hopes of those who had been pressing for complete empire free trade. Even so Britain's trade with the Dominions increased considerably after 1932 and certainly the trade agreements increased the amount of imperial cohesion.

e) Britain's Relations with the Dominions

By 1939 the Dominions were largely independent of Britain. This was especially true of Ireland. For ten years after the 1922 settlement, the government of the Irish Free State had generally cooperated with Britain. But in 1932 the Fianna Fail became the largest party in the Dail. De Valera, Fianna Fail's leader, made little secret of the fact that he wanted to create a united and independent Ireland. Almost immediately a series of issues, both constitutional and financial, were raised. By the end of 1932 Britain and Ireland were locked in a 'trade war', both countries increasing duties against goods from the other. In 1937 a new Irish Constitution laid claim to all 32 counties of Ireland and described Southern Ireland, or Eire, as 'a sovereign, independent, democratic state'. Britain and Southern Ireland did reach agreement over a number of issues in 1938, but Eire remained a member of the commonwealth in name only.

In South Africa the coming to power of the largely Afrikaner (or Boer) Nationalist Party in 1924 caused problems for Britain. Many Boers were anti-British and anxious to assert their national independence. Underlying many of the tensions was the fact that Britain was thought to be 'going soft' on native questions in her own African colonies. Relations between Britain and South Africa continued to be uneasy throughout the inter-war years.

Before 1914 Canada had been very loyal to Britain. But improved American-Canadian relations after 1918 lessened the need for close ties with Britain. Canadian politics were affected by divisions between the French- and English-speaking communities. Mackenzie King, Canadian Prime Minister for most of the inter-war period, depended on the support of the French-Canadians and was less pro-British than previous Canadian leaders had been.

Australia and New Zealand were more friendly to Britain, partly because of the increasing threat from Japan. Strong Anglo-Australian ties even survived the 1932-3 English cricket tour of Australia, when the English team (in a positively Australian determination to win the Ashes) resorted to body-line bowling!

f) Loyalty to the Mother Country

Although the formal bonds of Empire disappeared, many people in the Dominions still felt attached to Britain by ties of sentiment – a common past, a common language, similar institutions and common loyalty to the Royal Family. Most British emigrants still went to the Dominions (the British government spent about £6,000,000 encouraging emigration to the Dominions in the 1920s) and most British families had relatives and friends in the dominions. Recent emigrants continued to speak and think of Britain as home. The Dominions were also bound to Britain by ties of self-interest. In material terms Britain remained a vital market and an important source of capital.

Proof of the continuing importance of the Commonwealth connec-came in 1939. Britain declared war on Germany on 3 September. Mr Menzies of Australia immediately announced that when Britain was at war, so was Australia. In New Zealand there was an equally immediate response. Canada waited only until 7 September, the four-day delay being necessary to secure parliamentary approval. Although some French Canadians opposed the war, the vast majority of Canadians supported Britain. In South Africa the Afrikaner Nationalist Party supported a policy of neutrality; but General Smuts forced a debate in the House of Assembly and won enough Afrikaner votes to secure a majority for war, by 80 votes to 67. The General became Premier and on most wartime issues got his way. Only Eire stood for neutrality which she maintained throughout the war.

3 India

a) The Situation in 1919

The main imperial struggle that occurred between 1919 and 1945 was in

India, Britain's largest and most important colony. The loss of India – and the Indian army – would have a far-reaching effect on Britain's prestige and power. The main problem after 1918 was that a growing number of Indians wanted independence from Britain.

In 1919 most of India was controlled by Britain. British governments appointed a Secretary of State for India, who ruled from London, and a Viceroy, who ruled in India (after consultation with London!) Day-to-day administration was largely controlled by people of British origin. In 1921 there were about 150,000 Europeans living in India, ruling a native population of 250 million.

The British Raj, with its large army and magnificent state pageantry, was outwardly impressive. But the reality was somewhat different. Although there were ten provinces under direct British administration, much of India was still ruled by Indian princes with whom the British had treaties. Few Indians ever saw a British official. Throughout all India the problems of acute poverty and ignorance were massive.

Ultimately British authority rested on the Indian army, commanded by British officers and supported by British troops. The army had two main concerns: it had to defend India from the threats of invasion; and it had to maintain internal security. The main external threats came from Afghanistan, Russia and (later) Japan. This did not amount to much in the inter-war period. An Afghan invasion in 1919 was easily defeated. Russian – communist – ideas were a greater danger than Russian soldiers. Japan became a serious threat only after 1941. The North-west Frontier, where tribal rebellion was endemic, had long been the main internal trouble-spot. But from 1918 the army also had to deal with growing unrest within India, as more and more Indians demanded self-government.

Agitation for 'home rule' had begun to grow before 1914, particularly amongst Indian intellectuals. The Indian National Congress Party, formed in the 1880s, supported independence for India. But Congress members at first had little in common and little contact with the mass of India's population. Moreover many Indian Muslims were suspicious of self-government because they had no wish to be ruled by the Hindu majority. Such was the strength of this feeling that a specifically Muslim party – the Muslim League – had been founded in 1906. In 1914, therefore, the foundations of British power in India seemed firm enough and India had entered the First World War as a loyal member of the British Empire. Large numbers of Indians volunteered to serve the King-Emperor and fought on the Western Front and in the Middle East. But as the war dragged on, imperial fervour waned and political concessions were demanded as the price for continued support. Congress's support grew and it joined forces with the Muslim League in the cause of Indian independence.

Many Britons found it impossible to treat people of an alien culture and with different coloured skin as equals. Although the British had accepted that educated Indians were entitled to join in the administration of their own country, few people believed that India was ready for real democracy. But faced with a growing opposition, the Secretary of State for India, Edwin Montagu, in a speech to the Commons in 1917, announced that the British government supported:

1 the increasing association of Indians in every branch of the administration, and the gradual development of self-governing institutions, with a view to the progressive realisation of responsible government in India as an integral part of the British Empire.

The 1919 Government of India Act was framed to give substance to Montagu's declaration of policy. Elected Indians were allowed some power to determine policy, but only on non-contentious issues and only at provincial level. The Viceroy was left in control of important matters, such as defence, and was given power to legislate by decree for six months in the case of an emergency. This did not satisfy Indian nationalists who wanted nothing less than full-scale independence. Congress leaders advocated a policy of passive resistance as a way of bringing pressure to bear on British authority.

b) Gandhi and Passive Resistance

The man most associated with passive resistance is Mahatma Gandhi. Gandhi had qualified as a barrister in London and had once been a loyal supporter of the Raj. But his experiences as a lawyer defending Indians in South Africa exposed him to racism in its most blatant form and he became convinced that the rule of the white man in India should end. When he returned to India in 1915 he joined the Congress Party and soon became one of its most effective leaders. He never wavered in his devotion to the cause of Indian independence. He was equally committed to non-violent protest, devising and instigating new methods of civil disobedience to disrupt British rule. Civil disobedience techniques included days of fasting and prayer when all work and trade ceased, refusal to pay taxes, boycotting of British goods and the deliberate flouting of the law to court imprisonment. There was sometimes a strong element of coercion in such tactics and they could, and often did, spill over into violence. In consequence Gandhi was often seen as a hypocrite by many British officials. But Gandhi remained faithful to his principles and was an inspired and inspiring leader in the eyes of the majority of Hindus.

However, it is probable that Gandhi's influence on events has frequently been exaggerated. The history of the Indian independence movement is too complex to be explained by the ideas and activities of a single leader. There were many other Indian nationalist leaders and Gandhi's influence, even in Congress, was far from paramount. Perhaps his greatest importance was his appeal to the masses. Certainly in the last decade of his life (he was assassinated in 1948) he was the key negotiator and the British, the Muslims and all other political groups had to deal with him.

c) Amritsar

In 1918–19 India was far from calm. There were economic problems and a world-wide influenza epidemic killed millions of Indians. Fearing Bolshevik plots and faced with the threat of disorder, the Indian government passed the Rowlatt Acts, giving provincial governors the power to imprison without trial, and providing for trials without juries of anyone suspected of subversion. These Acts were met with a wave of protests. The most serious disturbances were in the Punjab region, especially in the city of Amritsar where several Europeans were killed in rioting.

The Governor of the Punjab, fearing that the region was on the verge of a major revolt, called on the army to restore order. On 13 April 1919, in defiance of a ban on public meetings, a large crowd assembled. Without warning, soldiers were ordered by General Dyer to fire on the illegal assembly. 379 people were killed and 1,200 were wounded.

Congress, not surprisingly, was highly critical of the Amritsar Massacre. An embarrassed British Government set up an official enquiry which criticised Dyer for ordering the firing without warning and for allowing the shooting to continue longer than was necessary. Dyer was relieved of his command and sent home on sick-leave. He claimed that he had acted out of duty and the Governor of the Punjab maintained that Dyer's action had averted much worse disorders. Although the government's treatment of Dyer was approved by the Commons, a House of Lords motion deplored the injustice shown to him. Many saw him as the 'saviour of India' and a fund to pay his defence costs raised £26,000.

Congress's campaign of civil disobedience gathered momentum – to the further embarrassment of the British. British rule was supposed to be beneficent. It did not seem so when masses of people protested and when Indians were shot or imprisoned without trial.

d) Talk of Reform

Passive and violent resistance continued on a large-scale throughout the 1920s, but order was slowly re-established and the 1919 Act was finally brought into operation. India now had greater autonomy and British officials who still effectively ruled the country did so in a way that was less dependent on London. But Lord Birkenhead, the new Secretary of State for India, had no faith in the Indian capacity for self-government. In 1927 he ordered a review of the workings of the 1919 Act. This task was entrusted to a commission, led by Sir John Simon, which was a parliamentary body and had no Indian members. This provoked widespread protest, and meetings of the commission were accompanied by demonstrations and riots throughout India. The commission finally recommended responsible government for India, but only at the provincial level.

In 1929 the Viceroy, Lord Irwin (later known as Lord Halifax), after consulting the newly-elected Labour government in Britain, decided that a conciliatory gesture was needed. He announced that Dominion status was the 'natural issue of India's constitutional progress' and suggested that a Round Table Conference, with Indian as well as British members, be held to discuss India's future. Churchill and other Conservatives were highly critical of the pledge of Dominion status. Churchill found himself at odds with Baldwin, the Conservative leader, and resigned from the shadow cabinet on the issue. By the time the National Government was formed in 1931, Churchill was so deeply at odds with the leading men in the Conservative Party that he was not included in the new administration or in any administration until after the outbreak of war in 1939.

Ironically, the Congress Party also had little confidence in Irwin's proposals. Congress leaders boycotted the Round Table talks, and embarked on a new campaign of civil disobedience. Gandhi's 241-mile march to the sea in 1930 to make salt (without paying the unpopular salt tax) attracted great attention. After his arrest, all followers of Congress felt called on to break the salt laws. There were outbreaks of violence in many parts of India.

In 1930 the first session of the Round Table Conference opened in London but made little headway. In January 1931 Gandhi was released. After intricate discussions with Irwin, he agreed to try to end the civil disobedience campaign and to attend the next session of the Round Table Conference. Many British imperialists were angry at Irwin's 'deal' with Gandhi. Gandhi's discarding of European dress when he met the viceroy was seen as a dramatic gesture of disrespect to the British Raj. Churchill commented:

1 In my opinion we ought to dissociate ourselves in the most public and formal manner from any complicity in the weak, wrong-headed and most unfortunate administration of India by the Socialists and by the Viceroy acting upon their responsibility. It is
5 alarming and also nauseating to see Mr Gandhi, a seditious Middle Temple lawyer, now posing as a fakir of a type well known in the East, striding half-naked up the steps of the viceregal palace, while he is still organising and conducting a defiant campaign of civil disobedience, to parley on equal terms
10 with the representatives of the King-Emperor. Such a spectacle can only increase the unrest in India and the danger to which

white people there are exposed. It can only encourage all the
forces which are hostile to British authority. What good can
possibly come of such extrordinary negotiations? Gandhi has said
15 within the last few weeks that he demands the substance of
independence, though he kindly adds that the British may keep
the shadow . . . These are his well-known aims. Surely they form
a strange basis for heart-to-heart discussions – 'sweet' we are told
they were – between this malignant, subversive fanatic and the
20 Viceroy of India.

In September 1931 the second session of the Round Table Conference met, with Gandhi in attendance. Little was achieved and Gandhi
returned to India to find a new and less sympathetic Viceroy. He was
soon involved in another civil disobedience campaign and re-arrested.
Firm government action, including the arrest of thousands of Congress
supporters, resulted in the quick collapse of the civil disobedience
campaign. The worldwide slump in agricultural prices had a dramatic
effect on the Indian peasantry who were now more concerned with
rents and interest rates than home rule.

Sam Hoare. ''Ullo mate! So you done a elephant too?'
**Winston. 'Ah! But my composition's different – an' I've made a lot more
o' the background.'** *Punch Cartoon by Bernard Partridge, 1933*

e) The 1935 Government of India Act

The British government was determined that some progress should be made towards Dominion status. Over the next four years a long and complicated measure, the Government of India Bill, laboriously made its way through all its parliamentary stages. Sir Samuel Hoare, the Secretary of State for India, played an important role in steering the bill through parliament. In January 1935 he made a radio broadcast:

1 The final test of our policy is whether it is one for the better government of India. This is the broad question that contains within it the issue that is constantly in our minds, the future welfare of the Indian masses. The millions of toiling workers
5 cannot be treated as an isolated part of the population that has no connection with the rest. I certainly do not suggest that self-government is, in itself, preferable to good government. Such a suggestion would be entirely inconsistent with the record of our rule in India. But I do maintain that the old system of paternal
10 government, great as have been its achievements on behalf of the Indian masses in the past, is no longer sufficient. However good it has been, it cannot survive a century of western education, a long period of free speech and of a free press and our deliberate policy of developing parliamentary government. We have reached the
15 point where the welfare of the people depends upon co-operation between the government and the political elements of the country.

Churchill was one of the main Conservative opponents of the bill. In February 1935 he said in parliament:

1 We have as good a right to be in India as anyone there except, perhaps, the depressed classes, who are the original stock. Our government is not an irresponsible government. It is a government responsible to the Crown and to parliament. It is incompa-
5 rably the best government that India has ever seen or ever will see. It is not true to say that the Indians, whatever their creed, would not rather have their affairs dealt with in many cases by British courts and British officers than by their own people, especially their own people of the opposite religion . . . We are
10 confronted with the old choice of self-government versus good government. We are invited to believe that the worst self-government is better than the best good government. That is going too far . . . [British] protection and security cannot be removed from India. They have grown with our growth and
15 strengthened with our strength. They will diminish with our diminution and decay with our decay . . . In so far as they are

withdrawn and this external aid withheld, India will descend not quite into the perils of Europe but into the squalor and anarchy of India in the sixteenth and seventeenth centuries.

Despite much Conservative opposition, the India bill finally received royal assent in 1935. The new act envisaged an all-India federation which would include the princely states. A national legislature would come into operation when over half the Indian princes joined the federation. There would be an elected Indian parliament but the British viceroy would continue to be head of state, retaining powers over defence and foreign affairs and the right to act on his own initiative in an emergency. The act gave significant powers to Indian politicians by establishing provincial governments – elected by a much wider franchise than before – in which ministers responsible to the legislature controlled all aspects of the administration.

The 1935 Government of India Act was attacked in Britain for going too far and in India for not going far enough. In Churchill's view, it marked 'the definite decline and even disappearance of our authority in India'. The Indian nationalist Subhas Chandra Bose said, 'It was a scheme not for self-government, but for maintaining British rule'. Gandhi was equally critical: 'India is still a prison, but the superintendant allows the prisoners to elect the officers who run the jail'. Historians have similarly varied views. Some see the act as being too little, too late. Others, however, regard it as a sensible compromise and a move in the right direction.

Congress, although critical of the act, decided to allow party members to contest elections to the provincial legislatures and Congress ministries were formed in a majority of the provinces. But problems remained. No progress was made towards the creation of a legislature at the centre because the princes could not agree terms on which to join the proposed federation. Although more Indians were admitted into the civil service, the Viceroy continued to have the final say. Britain had still not resigned itself to India becoming a totally independent country. Indeed in the late 1930s it seemed essential that India remain under British influence to contribute to the defence of a world system increasingly threatened by Germany and Japan.

f) The Outbreak of the Second World War

When war broke out in 1939, the Viceroy Lord Linlithgow, without consulting Indian leaders, announced that India was at war. Congress was divided on how to respond to the war. Gandhi was a pacifist and consistently opposed any support for the British war effort. Others sympathised with Britain but insisted that support could only be given in return for real constitutional advance. Some nationalists believed Britain's plight was India's opportunity and were prepared to work with Germany and Japan. In the end Congress leaders refused support for the war effort unless India could participate as an independent state and called on all the Congress provincial governments to resign office. This mass resignation was hailed as 'a day of deliverance' by Mohammed Ali Jinnah, leader of the Muslim League. He pledged Muslim support for the British cause and urged Muslims to join the British army. He hoped to win British support for a separate and independent Muslim state of Pakistan.

4 British Dependencies

In 1919 there were some 80 British colonies or dependencies – those territories whose connections with Britain rested not on colonisation by British settlers but on rule by a small number of British officials, ultimately controlled by the Colonial Office in London. These territories, scattered across the globe (see the map on page 46), formed an extraordinarily mixed collection. In many cases the population was small. In most cases the economy was primitive. The solidarity of the British officials often provided such unity as the dependencies possessed.

Most Britons assumed that the colonies would one day evolve into independent members of a multi-racial Commonwealth. However, little progress was made in this direction between the wars. In most colonies there seemed little pressure for 'home rule' and Britain kept order with relative ease. Without pressure from below, it was unlikely that Britain would grant independence. The colonies were thought to be too valuable to be voluntarily given up. Moreover, racial prejudice and the habit of authority made it difficult for many colonial officials to take seriously the idea of non-Europeans governing themselves. The only colonial people to be granted self-rule were the 30,000 white settlers in Southern Rhodesia who ruled over 1,000,000 blacks. Even Labour MPs believed that the aim of self-determination was not realistic in many dependencies for a long time to come. Thus there was a sense of stability in colonial affairs between the wars.

The 1920s and 1930s were the heyday of the Colonial Service, which took much of the 'cream' of the public schools and universities. Colonial governors had considerable freedom and often acted without reference to London. However, the character of British rule in the dependencies tends to be misunderstood. It is often seen as despotism exercised by pompous or bigoted sahibs in white shorts and pith helmets. Or (less fashionably) it is depicted as a selfless struggle against the poverty and ignorance of the primitive masses.

However, in reality the number of British officials was so small and the financial resources of most colonies so slim that colonial rule had to rely upon locally recruited subordinates to man both its bureaucracy and its security forces. British officials were often forced to co-operate with native leaders who remained the main source of authority in the countryside. This policy of 'indirect rule' was in general favour between the wars. It had a number of advantages. Not only was it cheap, but it also meant that British officials sometimes escaped blame for policies for which they were ultimately responsible.

In the inter-war years relatively little money was spent on colonial economic development, education, public health or scientific research. It had long been official government policy that colonies should be financially self-supporting. Most private lenders thought there were safer investments elsewhere. Not much was done, therefore, to fulfil what Britain claimed was her 'positive trust' to her colonial subjects. A governor of Tanganyika described his colony as 'lying in mothballs' between the wars, and this is an appropriate description for what happened in many dependencies. A West Indian Royal Commission which reported in 1939 was very critical of the inertia of imperial rule. Few colonies experienced much in the way of economic prosperity and most suffered severely from the world depression of the 1930s.

5 The Middle East

a) British Influence

Britain had important interests in the Middle East before the First World War. The security of the Suez Canal, the 'lifeline' of the Empire, was a fundamental objective of British policy, and the recent discovery of oil had made the region increasingly important economically. By 1914 Britain controlled Aden and Cyprus and had considerable influence over Egypt and many of the smaller Sheikdoms and Sultanates of the Persian Gulf. The First World War greatly extended the British interest. By the end of 1918 Turkey had lost control of all its Arab territories. It was unclear how this political vacuum should be filled. Despite the vague promises made to Arab leaders in the war, few British politicians supported T.E. Lawrence (of Arabia) who dreamed of Arab states becoming 'our first brown dominions and not our last brown colonies'. The lands lying between the Mediterranean and Persia were finally divided into British and French spheres of influence. France was given a mandate over Syria. Britain took over the administration of Palestine and Trans-Jordan.

Between the wars Britain was to be the dominant power in the Middle East. However, Britain's position depended upon the careful management of Anglo-Arab relations. Interference with local society was generally kept to a minimum, for Britain was anxious not to arouse a full-scale Arab revolt. Control was generally exerted through friendly local rulers who depended for their survival, in the last resort, on British military assistance.

b) Egypt, Iraq and Trans-Jordan

Britain's main aim in Egypt was to maintain the security of the Suez Canal. Serious demonstrations in 1919 convinced many British officials that Britain's 1914 annexation of Egypt could not be made permanent. A treaty was signed in 1922 under which Egypt's independence was recognised and the Sultan became King Fuad I. But Britain still effectively controlled Egypt's foreign and defence policies and kept an army in the country to do so. In 1936 a further treaty gave Egypt control over its own army, but authorised the presence of 10,000 British troops in the Suez Canal Zone and allowed the return of British troops to Egypt in unlimited numbers in times of emergency.

In 1918 the whole of Mesopotamia (or Iraq) was effectively under British military rule. However, many Muslims had no wish to be under British control and in 1920 a revolt was suppressed only with difficulty. When Winston Churchill became Colonial Secretary in 1921, his first concern was to reduce the costs of administering Iraq. He determined to find an Arab ruler who would be acceptable to the people of Iraq and friendly to Britain. Churchill supported Feisal, third son of Sherif Hussein of Mecca, an Arab leader whom Britain had supported during the First World War. Although Feisal had no previous connection with the area, he was duly 'elected' King of Iraq. In 1922 a treaty was signed under which Iraq became an independent state bound to Britain during the period of the mandate. The internal security of the country largely rested with the RAF which assisted Feisal's government to bring order to troublesome regions. The mandate formally ended in 1930, but Iraq accepted the presence of British military bases and remained a political client of Britain throughout the 1930s and 1940s.

Feisal's brother, Abdullah, was made ruler of the largely desert kingdom of Trans-Jordan which remained relatively tranquil under the mandate.

c) Palestine

Palestine was to pose a tremendous problem for Britain in the inter-war years. In 1917 the Balfour Declaration had promised Britain's support for the 'establishment in Palestine of a national home for the Jewish people'. The Declaration was issued with the interests of the Jewish people in mind and with the object of winning support from Jewish opinion in the USA for the allied war-effort. It was deliberately vague. What was to be the exact status of a national home? What were to be its frontiers? A further and greater problem which was left unanswered was how to reconcile Jewish immigration into an area where the vast majority of people were Arabs.

Perhaps the easiest option would have been for Britain to have washed its hands of the whole Palestinian problem at the end of the

First World War. Balfour himself saw no reason for a British presence in Palestine and would have preferred the USA to have become the mandatory power. However, most British politicians were pleased to be given control of Palestine. They recognised the strategic importance of the area in safeguarding the eastern flank of the Suez Canal. Britain, therefore, was left with the task of governing Palestine and attempting to reconcile the conflicting demands of the Arabs and the Jews.

On the whole politicians in Britain sympathised with the Jewish desire to have a country of their own, and some even envisaged a Jewish-colonised Palestine becoming a 'cornerstone' of the British Commonwealth. However, most British officials in the Middle East tended to sympathise with the Arabs who did not wish to see Jews taking over their land. The Jews and their supporters effectively won the day. By 1925 there had been considerable Jewish immigration into Palestine and many Jews made no secret of their intention to turn the 'national home' into a Jewish nation state.

Jewish immigration caused increasing Arab resentment and in 1929 there were serious anti-Jewish riots. In 1930 a White Paper proposed a limit on future Jewish immigration, but it aroused so much opposition in pro-Jewish circles in Britain and America that no further action was taken on its recommendations.

With the coming to power of Hitler in 1933 and the consequent persecution of German Jews, the pressure to increase Jewish immigration became irresistible. Palestine was now seen as a sanctuary as well as a homeland. Increased immigration provoked increased Arab opposition. The Arab majority in Palestine wanted to see the establishment of an independent Arab state and an end to Jewish immigration. In 1936 a serious Arab revolt broke out, directed as much against British and moderate Arab leaders as against the Jews. It lasted for the next three years and Britain had to send large numbers of troops to Palestine in order to keep control.

In 1937 the Peel Commission recommended that partition of Palestine into an Arab state and a Jewish state (with a British buffer zone) was the only answer. However, it proved impossible to devise a workable plan of partition, and attempts to persuade Arabs and Jews to discuss the problem also ended in failure.

In 1939 a further White Paper abandoned the idea of partition, which was unpopular with the Arabs. Instead Britain considered the idea of independence for a federated Palestinian state. In the meantime, Jewish immigration was limited to 10,000 a year for five years, with an additional 25,000 in the first year. Thereafter no further immigration would be allowed without Arab approval. This would preserve an Arab majority in Palestine for the foreseeable future. With war in Europe brewing, Britain was anxious not to alienate Arab opinion.

d) Conclusion

Before 1939 Britain's position in the Middle East was far from secure. Germany and Italy encouraged unrest among the Arabs, many of whom wanted an end to British influence. However, pre-1939 Britain was reasonably confident that she could preserve her dominance in the region. It was assumed that tactful diplomacy would defuse Arab nationalism and that the Arabs would always be divided.

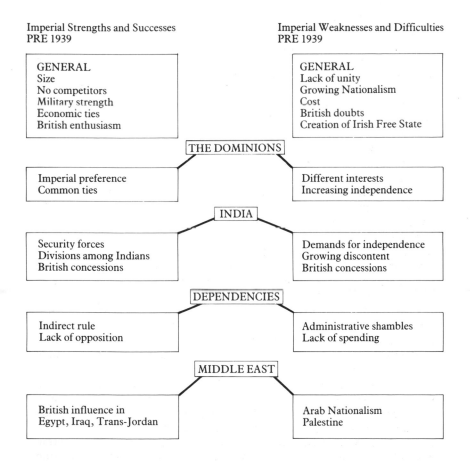

Imperial Strengths and Successes
PRE 1939

Imperial Weaknesses and Difficulties
PRE 1939

GENERAL
Size
No competitors
Military strength
Economic ties
British enthusiasm

GENERAL
Lack of unity
Growing Nationalism
Cost
British doubts
Creation of Irish Free State

THE DOMINIONS

Imperial preference
Common ties

Different interests
Increasing independence

INDIA

Security forces
Divisions among Indians
British concessions

Demands for independence
Growing discontent
British concessions

DEPENDENCIES

Indirect rule
Lack of opposition

Administrative shambles
Lack of spending

MIDDLE EAST

British influence in
Egypt, Iraq, Trans-Jordan

Arab Nationalism
Palestine

Summary – The Empire 1919–39

Making notes on 'The Empire 1919–39'

You need to remember that the Empire was essential to Britain if she was to be a great world power, and that the Dominions, colonies and dependencies, and mandated territories in the Middle East were all seen as part of the Empire. Historians disagree about whether the Empire was in irreversible decline or at its height in the inter-war years. It is important that your notes are organised to give you a clear grasp of the main arguments and debates. How strong – or weak – was the Empire in the period 1919–39?

Answering essay questions on 'The Empire, 1919–39'

Questions on British imperial policy in the period 1919–39 are likely to fall into three categories: India; the Dominions; and the Empire in general. Here are some examples:

1 'Amritsar, civil disobedience, the India Act, were stepping stones to the relinquishment of British rule in India.' Discuss this statement.
2 Why did relationships with the Dominions assume such importance for British governments in the period from 1914 to 1939?
3 To what extent was the British Empire in irreversible decline in the period 1919–39?

Question 1 asks you to focus on India. You will need to say something about developments in India from the Amritsar Massacre in 1919 to the 1935 India Act. But unless you are very careful the danger is that you will end up writing a narrative essay rather than an analytical one. You must remember to answer the question. Do you agree with the quote? What would your conclusion be?

Question 2 is difficult. You need to put Britain's relationships with the dominions into the context of British foreign policy as a whole in the period from the start of the First World War to the start of the Second World War. Why were the dominions important for Britain? What happened to Britain's relationships with the dominions in this period?

You should be far better prepared for question 3! The main difficulty might be deciding what to include and what to miss out. Plan an answer to the question, listing the main points you would make in your paragraphs. What would be your conclusion – and why?

Source-based questions on 'The Empire, 1919–39'

1 The 1926 Balfour Report

Read the extracts from Leo Amery's diary on page 53. Answer the following questions:

a) Explain why Winston Churchill and Cave were opposed to the Balfour Report. (**2 marks**)
b) What exactly was Amery's 'modern conception of Empire'? (**2 marks**)
c) Why do you think Amery regarded the Balfour Report as so important? (**3 marks**)
d) What did Amery mean when he wrote, 'It all makes the need for an Imperial economic policy more urgent than ever'? (**3 marks**)

2 Churchill on Gandhi in 1931

Read Churchill's comments on Gandhi on pages 59–60. Answer the following questions:

a) Why did Churchill describe Gandhi as 'a seditious Middle Temple lawyer'? (**2 marks**)
b) Why was Churchill critical of Gandhi's meeting with the Viceroy? (**4 marks**)
c) Account for Churchill's criticism of Gandhi? (**4 marks**)
d) How might a Government representative have answered Churchill's question: 'What good can possibly come of such extraordinary negotiations?' (**5 marks**)

3 The 1935 India Bill

Read the comments of Hoare and Churchill on the India Bill (pages 61–2), and study the Punch cartoon reproduced on page 60. Answer the following questions:

a) Comment on the date of the cartoon (in comparison with the date of the two speeches). (**3 marks**)
b) What point was the cartoon trying to make? (**4 marks**)
c) On what points might Hoare and Churchill have agreed? (**5 marks**)
d) On what points did they disagree? (**5 marks**)
e) What was Hoare's main justification for the India Bill? (**3 marks**)

CHAPTER 4

The Gathering Storm 1931–6

1 Depression and Disarmament

a) Depression

At the start of the 1930s, there seemed every chance that the peace and stability of the 1920s might continue. There were some problems but they did not seem particularly dangerous. No-one seriously contemplated the possibility of a major war. But from 1931 there were to be increasing threats to international peace. Many arose from the effects of the terrible world-wide economic depression that followed the 1929 Wall Street Crash.

Britain was hit hard by the depression. The coal, textiles, shipbuilding, and iron and steel industries were all badly affected. Trade fell by 40 per cent. By 1932 over 20 per cent of the British work force was unemployed. The search for economic recovery eclipsed everything else, including foreign policy. Ramsay MacDonald's Labour government clung firmly to orthodox economics, cutting government spending and trying to balance the budget. In 1931 a massive financial crisis loomed; confidence in sterling sagged and Britain was forced to come off the Gold Standard. The Labour Cabinet split on the question of unemployment pay cuts. In an effort to save the economy, MacDonald split the Labour Party and joined forces with the opposition in a National Government. In October 1931 a general election was called and the electors were asked to give the National Government a free hand to deal with the crisis situation.

The National Government gained the biggest majority in modern history – 554 MPs against 61 for all the other groups combined. The Conservatives won 473 seats – over 75 per cent of the House of Commons. The pattern of British politics had been massively altered. There was no credible alternative government. MacDonald remained Prime Minister, but the National Government was essentially Conservative and increasingly dominated by Stanley Baldwin, the Tory leader, and Neville Chamberlain, the Chancellor of the Exchequer.

British leaders would have preferred international co-operation to bring about world economic recovery since Britain was so dependent on world trade. However, the Depresssion encouraged all countries to think primarily of themselves. In order to protect her own industries, Britain finally abandoned free trade and turned to Empire protection. The Import Duties Act of February 1932 imposed a 10 per cent tax on most imported goods, except those from the British Empire. The Ottawa Conference in July 1932 led to Britain and the Dominions agreeing to establish an imperial economic bloc, protecting their trade

by a system of quotas and tariffs against countries outside the Commonwealth (see page 47).

b) Disarmament

The National Government, committed to restoring sound finances, was
reluctant to maintain defence expenditure. Many, particularly on the
left, saw no point in spending money on armaments, believing they
were more likely to cause a war rather than to prevent one. Indeed most
Labour and Liberal politicians rejected the use of force as an instrument of policy, pressed for disarmament as the chief element in British
foreign policy, and developed their opposition to the National Government mainly on this issue.

Throughout the 1920s there had been an increasing spate of anti-war
literature – poems, plays and autobiographies – condemning the futility
and wastefulness of the First World War. A host of anti-war organisa-
tions – the National Peace Council, the League of Nations Union and
the Peace Pledge Union – sprang up and seemed to be gaining in
strength. In October 1933 in the East Fulham by-election, a Conservative candidate who advocated an increase in defence spending was
defeated by a pacifist Labour opponent. The Conservative majority of
over 14,000 was transformed into a Labour majority of nearly 5,000.
Even the public schools seemed to be turning out pacifists. In 1933 the
Oxford Union resolved by 257 votes to 153 that 'this house will not fight
for King and Country'.

The National Government, intending to ward off Labour and Liberal
attack, strongly adhered to the principles of disarmament and international co-operation through the League of Nations. Almost all politicians – Conservative, Labour and Liberal – regarded the League as an
alternative to armaments. No one believed in re-arming in order to
support the League of Nations. It was assumed that goodwill and
enlightened opinion, plus the threat of economic sanctions, would deter
potential aggressors.

MacDonald pinned great hopes on the World Disarmament Conference which met at Geneva in February 1932. Arthur Henderson, a
Labour colleague and ex-British Foreign Secretary, was the conference
president. The main problem from the start was Germany's claim for
parity of treatment. Britain was prepared to accept this claim, but
France, the strongest military power in Europe, still feared Germany,
and French leaders were not prepared to reduce their forces without
watertight guarantees of security. To most Frenchmen it seemed as if
'equality of rights' meant that Germany would be able to rearm and
again threaten to attack them. It proved impossible to find a compromise between the German demand for equality and the French demand
for security.

c) Increasing Problems

Despite failure on the disarmament front, MacDonald continued to hope that the just grievances of Germany could be settled by negotiation. Given Germany's dreadful economic position (over 5,000,000 unemployed in 1932), most British MPs felt that reparations should be cancelled. In June 1932 a conference under the presidency of MacDonald met at Lausanne. This conference succeeded in settling the reparations problem. Germany agreed to make a final payment of 2.6 million marks to a European Reconstruction Fund. In return German reparation payments would be abolished.

This was one of the last successes of the collective diplomacy which had prevailed for much of the 1920s. This had tended to favour the maintenance of the status quo and thus had suited British interests. But in the early 1930s Britain's international position began to deteriorate rapidly. The world-wide depression had different effects in different countries. It made some countries more peaceful than ever. But in others it undermined democracy and led to governments coming to power which favoured war and foreign conquest as a means of acquiring new lands, markets and raw materials to help alleviate the economic situation. As a result the international climate became increasingly threatening and Britain faced potential challenges from Japan, Germany and Italy. Trust in disarmament and collective security, and the consequent cut-back in military spending, meant that Britain was not best prepared for the dangers that lay ahead.

2 The Problem of Japan

By the 1920s Japan was a major economic, military and imperial power. She had secured Formosa from China in 1895, Korea from Russia in 1905, and after 1914 had taken all German colonies in China and the Pacific north of the Equator. She also had substantial interests in Manchuria, a large province which she leased from China.

Japan was nominally a constitutional monarchy, under the Emperor Hirohito, and for most of the 1920s had been governed by a succession of liberal coalitions. Most of these governments supported international co-operation and favoured peaceful resolutions of conflicts between nations. But many Japanese had been disappointed by their gains from the First World War and favoured expansion. The turmoil in China and the often provocative policies of the Chinese government provided a permanent incitement to Japan to intervene.

The onset of the depression at the start of the 1930s hit Japan hard and was a powerful incentive to military adventure. Territorial expansion could provide the raw materials and markets she lacked. A growing number of radical nationalists, especially strong in the army, wanted Japan to pursue her own national interests and not be constrained by the 'rules' of the west. Assassinations of politicians who opposed the nationalist cause became an increasingly common phenomenon.

In September 1931 units in the Japanese army, acting without orders from their government, seized a number of points in Manchuria. Aware of popular support for the occupation of Manchuria, the Japanese government did little to halt the army. China immediately appealed to the League of Nations. Japan's action was the first real challenge by a major power to the 'new international system' and there was concern that Article 16 of the Covenant of the League might be invoked. This Article declared that if any member of the League should resort to war in disregard to its obligations, this would amount to an act of war against all other members of the League. The League was then empowered to subject the aggressor to immediate economic sanctions.

However, it was by no means clear that Japan had committed a 'resort to war' in an area where incidents between Chinese and Japanese soldiers were commonplace. Moreover, China did not immediately attempt to invoke Article 16 and so at first the League did little except appeal to China and Japan to refrain from action which might worsen the situation. But the Japanese army was in no mood to be coerced by verbal warnings from the League. By February 1932 it had occupied the whole of Manchuria and set up the puppet state of Manchukuo.

Britain was concerned with the developments in Manchuria. She had serious interests in the Far East – in Hong Kong, Malaya, Singapore, and Shanghai – and a military presence in the area. Most British politicians were critical of Japan's action, particularly when Chinese forces were attacked near Shanghai, and the British government was certainly not prepared to recognise Manchukuo. But there was also some sympathy for Japan. Anglo-Japanese relations had been friendly for many years. Japan, like Britain, had suffered considerable provocation from Chinese Nationalists throughout the 1920s. Much of China was in a state of political chaos. Japan had at least brought relative prosperity to the part of Manchuria she had previously controlled, might well restore order in the whole of Manchuria, and would certainly provide a bulwark against Bolshevik aggression.

Britain had more than enough domestic problems in 1931–2 and had no intention of risking a major war with Japan. British forces in the Far East were small and Singapore and Hong Kong were essentially undefended. An economic blockade was likely to achieve little. The British navy was not strong enough to enforce sanctions and the USA, Japan's biggest trading partner, made it clear she would not support any League action. As a result, Britain's main aim throughout the Manchuria crisis was to try to facilitate an agreement between Japan and China.

The League of Nations eventually set up a commisssion under Lord Lytton to inquire into the rights and wrongs of what had happened in Manchuria. Lytton spent many months in Manchuria and China before issuing his final report in October 1932. The Lytton Commission declared that many of the Japanese grievances were justified, but condemned Japan's methods of redressing those grievances. It recommended that Manchuria should have autonomous status under Chinese supervision. The League accepted Lytton's recommendations by 42 votes to 1. Japan, the only nation to vote against the recommendations, withdrew from the League in protest and ignored its rulings.

Britain condemned Japan's action but did little else. Given her weak military position, there was much to be said for caution. If action was to be taken, American support was vital – but that support was not forthcoming. Japanese imperialism was a potential threat to British interests in the Far East, and possibly even to India, Australia and New Zealand. But it was not an immediate threat. Indeed Japanese expansion in northern China could be seen as reducing the risk of Japanese expansion in other, more sensitive, areas. The best policy, therefore, seemed to be to accept Japan's take-over of Manchuria and to hope that the Japanese threat did not develop. A few limited precautions were taken. Work was resumed on the Singapore naval base and the so-called '10-Year Rule', the diplomatic and military assumption that no major war would occur in the next ten years, was abandoned. However, in practice, this meant very little. Britain did not yet embark on a serious programme of rearmament.

Some politicians, such as Neville Chamberlain, were keen to restore friendly relations with Japan as soon as possible, if needs be at the expense of China. This seemed a good way to protect British possessions and investments in the Far East. It might also reduce the amount of money that Britain would have to spend on improving her defences to combat Japan. But others realised that an Anglo-Japanese pact would have little moral justification, might further damage the prestige of the League of Nations, and would do untold damage to Britain's relations with China, the USSR and especially the USA.

Relations between Britain and Japan remained uneasy. Throughout the 1930s different military and political factions in Japan often pursued conflicting policies and Britain found it hard to accept that chaos and confusion, rather than duplicity, frequently lay behind the twists and turns of Japanese policy. But Japanese nationalists increasingly stressed that Japan regarded the whole of China and East Asia as her special sphere of influence. This was worrying. So was the fact that Japan made it clear that she intended to end the existing naval agreements and to increase her navy. The Anti-Comintern Pact, signed by Germany and Japan in November 1936, further alarmed Britain. The Pact was aimed primarily against the USSR, but might be a potential threat to Britain. British efforts to bring about some kind of reconciliation between China and Japan failed. Nevertheless the British government had no wish to alienate Japan unnecessarily and relations between Britain and Japan did improve in 1936 and early 1937.

3 The Problem of Germany 1933–5

a) Adolf Hitler

In 1933 Adolf Hitler came to power in Germany. This was a cause for alarm – if not panic – in many countries, not least Britain. It seemed certain that Hitler's Nazi government would challenge the existing European balance of power. But the exact nature of the problem was not easy to determine then – or now. Possible solutions to the threat posed by Hitler were, therefore, even more difficult to define.

Hitler was clearly intent on freeing Germany from the shackles of the Versailles settlement. He wanted to see an end to the restrictions on Germany's rearmament and her right to remilitarise the Rhineland. He also favoured the inclusion within Germany of all the German-speaking people in Europe, especially the Austrians and the Germans in Czechoslovakia and Poland. In his book *Mein Kampf*, written in the mid-1920's, he had also talked about winning *lebensraum*, or living space for Germany in the east, at the expense of Russia.

Was *Mein Kampf* an early folly or a blue-print for the future? Even assuming it was a blue-print, did Hitler actually pose a threat to Britain? In *Mein Kampf* he spoke of Britain as a potential ally of Germany. His main ambitions seemed to be in eastern not western Europe. His chief enemy seemed likely to be the USSR. The prospect of a German-Russian war was not necessarily a bad thing from the point of view of British interests. At the very least a stronger Germany would be a useful bulwark against Russian or Communist expansion.

Even today historians disagree about Hitler's ultimate intentions. In 1961 A.J.P. Taylor, in his book *The Origins of the Second World War*, claimed that Hitler was really a rather ordinary German statesman with a rather ordinary mission – that of increasing Germany's standing among the world's nations. He was no different to previous German leaders. He was a man who took advantage of situations as they arose and rarely took the initiative himself. He was no more wicked or unscrupulous than most other statesmen. A.J.P. Taylor was always prone to overstatement, and *The Origins of the Second World War* sparked off a great and at times bitter debate among historians. Few historians today accept Taylor's arguments in their entirety. Most probably think that Hitler had a clear and cold-blooded general purpose: overthrow Versailles; win *lebensraum* in eastern Europe; and make Germany the strongest power in Europe. But many now accept that Hitler had no detailed programme but simply improvised as events unfolded. Given the debates among historians about Hitler's objectives, it is hardly surprising that British politicians in the 1930s were unsure about how to deal with the new German leader.

There were certainly some who feared the worst. Sir Robert Vansittart, the leading civil servant at the Foreign Office, warned ministers from the start about the threat of Nazism. So too did Winston Churchill. They were not alone. A report from the Defence Requirements Committee concluded in 1934 that, 'We take Germany as the ultimate potential enemy against whom our long-range defensive policy must be directed'. But the fact that some people distrusted Hitler gave no one the right or power to intervene in Germany. Some hoped – and indeed expected – that Hitler would not last long. If he failed to solve Germany's economic problems, he might well lose power. Many believed that Hitler might well be sobered by holding office. Some British observers thought there was a limit to his ambitions. They were convinced he sought German equality rather than hegemony in Europe. There remained considerable sympathy for German grievances and many thought that greater efforts should be made to redress those grievances.

But there seemed to be no immediate German threat. It was assumed that it would take Hitler a long time to get Germany back on its feet. Some thought Britain should help Germany's economic recovery. This was a view particularly supported by the Bank of England and the Board of Trade. There would be considerable economic gains for Britain if Germany again became prosperous. The return of German prosperity might also help heal the wounds of the past and produce an atmosphere of international friendship and understanding. However, there was no agreement on what was the best British economic package for Germany.

b) Hitler's First Moves 1933–4

Hitler's first moves in foreign policy were relatively cautious. He certainly did not seem particularly hostile to Britain. He gave several interviews to British journalists and went out of his way to express admiration for Britain and its Empire and to voice the hope that 'the two great Germanic nations' could work together.

However, in October 1933 Germany withdrew from both the Disarmament Conference at Geneva and the League of Nations. Hitler's excuse was that the great powers would not treat Germany as an equal. This action effectively destroyed the Disarmament Conference. Without German participation, no useful agreement could be reached. Yet a long time would elapse before enthusiasts could admit to themselves that the Disarmament Conference was dead. Many hoped that Hitler might be persuaded to return to the Conference.

In 1933–4 most British MPs were aware that Germany was secretly rearming and thus becoming an increasing threat. In March 1934 Winston Churchill said in the House of Commons:

  1 We are, it is admitted, the fifth air power only – if that . . . Our nearest neighbour Germany is arming fast and no one is going to

'*Well – What are you going to do about it now?*' *Cartoon by David Low showing from left to right, Simon, Mussolini, Daladier and Hitler.*

stop her. That seems quite clear. No one proposes a preventive war to stop Germany breaking the Treaty of Versailles. She is
5 going to arm; she is doing it; she has been doing it. I have no knowledge of the details, but it is well known that those very gifted people with their science and with their factories – with what they call their 'Air-Sport' – are capable of developing with great rapidity the most powerful Air Force for all purposes,
10 offensive and defensive, within a very short period of time. I dread the day when the means of threatening the heart of the British Empire should pass into the hands of the present rulers of Germany. We should be in a position which would be odious to every man who values freedom of action and independence, and
15 also in a position of the utmost peril for our crowded, peaceful population engaged in their daily toil. I dread that day, but it is not perhaps far distant ... We want the measures to achieve parity. No nation playing the part we play and aspire to play in the world has a right to be in a position where it can be
20 blackmailed.

Sir John Simon, the Foreign Secretary, said:

1 German civil aviation is now the first in Europe. Germany already
  has in effect a fleet of 600 military aeroplanes and facilities for its
  very rapid expansion. She can already mobilise an army three
  times as great as that authorised by the Treaty and a rapid
5 expansion of her mobilisation facilities must be expected.

In the same year Baldwin told the Commons:

1 I think it is well for the man in the street to realise that there is no
  power on earth that can protect him from being bombed.
  Whatever people may tell him, the bomber will always get
  through. The only defence is offence, which means that you have
5 to kill more women and children more quickly than the enemy if
  you want to save yourselves. I just mention that so that people
  may realise what is waiting for them when the next war comes.

In 1934 Britain began to spend more money on the RAF. But few
people in Britain yet feared war. Indeed the Labour Party strongly
censured the Government for increasing spending on defence and thus
'jeopardising the prospects of international disarmament'. Nor did
Britain draw nearer to France. The British Cabinet, still suspicious of
French intentions, was not prepared to support Anglo-French staff
talks. The French, meanwhile, began to push ahead with the building
of the Maginot Line, the great line of defences down their border with
Germany.

Hitler continued to be cautious. In 1934, to the surprise of many of
his own followers, he signed a non-aggression pact with Poland. A
Nazi-inspired *putsch* in Austria in 1934 led to the assassination of the
Austrian Chancellor, Dollfuss. Mussolini regarded Austria as an Italian
satellite state and rushed 100,000 Italian troops to the Austrian border
as a warning in case Hitler tried to take advantage of the confusion in
Vienna. Mussolini's action enabled the Austrian authorities to stabilise
the internal situation. Hitler did nothing to help the Austrian Nazis and
their *putsch* failed.

c) Germany Rearms

In March 1935 Hitler declared that Germany had an air force and
announced the introduction of conscription, forbidden under the terms
of the Treaty of Versailles. The German army would be increased to
about 500,000 men – five times the permitted number. Although
everyone was aware that Germany had been violating the military
clauses of Versailles for many years, Hitler's announcement was a

diplomatic challenge which could not be ignored.

The heads of government and foreign ministers of Britain, France and Italy met at Stresa in April 1935. They condemned Hitler's action and resolved to maintain the existing treaty settlement of Europe and to resist any future attempt to change it by force. This agreement was known as the Stresa Front.

France also strengthened her ties with the USSR. In May 1935 France and Russia concluded a treaty of mutual assistance, although ratification was postponed for some time. This was reinforced by a Russian-Czechoslovakian agreement. It seemed as though Europe intended to stand firm against the German threat.

However, Britain did not consider herself to be particularly threatened by Hitler, who so far had said nothing about naval rearmament. In June 1935 Britain signed a Naval Agreement with Germany. By the terms of this Agreement the Germans were to have the right to build up to 35 per cent of Britain's capital ships and to be allowed parity in submarines in exceptional circumstances. This agreement, signed without prior discussion with France or Italy, damaged the Stresa Front. Britain, by sanctioning a much larger German navy than was permitted by the Treaty of Versailles, seemed to be condoning Germany's unilateral rearmament immediately after the Stresa Front's condemnation.

Although the Anglo-German Naval Agreement was criticised by some at the time and by many historians since, in 1935 it had the approval of the Admiralty, Foreign Office and the entire Cabinet. They thought the Naval Agreement was a realistic contribution to peace. The Disarmament talks had failed – largely through French stubborness. Many British politicians were angry at France's flirtation with Russia. The French seemed to be doing their best to encircle Germany, a move that might encourage rather than avert war. Moreover Britain, which still imported half its required foodstuffs, was anxious about its navy. Given the Japanese threat in the Far East, the British government had no wish to face a greater danger in home waters. The Agreement at least ensured that Britain maintained – and Germany accepted – a naval superiority twice as great as in 1914.

Hitler seems to have hoped that the Naval Agreement might lead to a fully-fledged alliance with Britain. However, it was clear that British public opinion would accept nothing in the nature of an Anglo-German alliance. Nazi dictatorship was unpopular in many quarters in Britain, especially on the left. But it was also clear that British public opinion would not approve using military force to overthrow Hitler. Germany now embarked on a serious rearmament programme. This meant that henceforward Hitler could not be stopped without the risk of a major war.

4 The Problem of Italy 1935–6

a) Anglo-Italian Relations before 1935

Before 1935 relations between Italy and Britain had been reasonably satisfactory. However, Mussolini's ambitions to build up an empire in Africa and make the Mediterranean an 'Italian lake' meant that there was certainly potential for Anglo-Italian rivalry. Britain had her own colonial interests in Africa, and the Mediterranean was seen as vital to British trade routes. In the early 1930s there was increasing trouble between Britain and Italy in the Red Sea, Libya and Egypt. The fact that Mussolini, like many Italians, felt that Italy had made inadequate gains in the First World War was also a potential problem. Italy tended to see herself as a 'have-not' power rather than a power committed to the preservation of the status quo. But for most of the 1920s and early 1930s Mussolini had done little to upset things and had generally sought prestige by remaining within the bounds of international society. In 1933 Britain saw Italy, along with France and the USA, as a friendly power against whom no major defence preparations were necessary.

Indeed many British and French politicians hoped that Mussolini might be a useful ally against Hitler. There was some basis for these hopes. Mussolini had met Hitler in 1934 and had not been impressed. Italy was every bit as anxious as France about what would happen if Germany once again became a major power in central Europe. In particular the prospect of a union between Germany and Austria, which would result in a powerful German state along her northern border, terrified Italy. Mussolini's swift action in sending troops to the Austrian border in 1934 had done more than anything to stop Hitler intervening in Austria on the side of the Austrian Nazis. In April 1935 Italy had joined with France and Britain in the Stresa Front.

However, by 1935 trouble was brewing. Mussolini wanted to increase the Italian Empire in Africa by taking over Abyssinia (now known as Ethiopia), one of the last countries in Africa which was free from European control. Italy had long had designs on Abyssinia. In 1896 an Italian army had been defeated at Adowa by the Abyssinians and all Italian prisoners had been castrated. Many Italians still wanted to avenge this humiliating defeat. In the early 1930s there were a number of incidents along the borders of Abyssinia and Italian Somaliland and Eritrea. As early as 1932 Italy began to make plans to take over Abyssinia. Mussolini believed that Italy needed more raw materials and living space for its rising population. Moreover a bold foreign policy might be a useful distraction from economic distress in Italy. In 1934 there was a skirmish between Italian and Abyssinia forces at the border water-holes at Wal Wal. This incident was not staged by

Mussolini but it gave him a convenient excuse to build up his forces and prepare for an attack in October 1935.

b) Events in 1935

Mussolini recognised that any advance in Africa might well damage Italian relations with Britain and France. Therefore, he made considerable diplomatic efforts to ensure that they would accept his Abyssinian adventure. In January 1935 Laval, the French Foreign Minister, visited Rome and in effect promised Mussolini a free hand in Abyssinia. The French were very anxious to keep on good terms with Italy because of the increasing German threat. It also seemed that Britain was prepared to accept Italian expansion. The British were well aware of the Italian military build-up in Africa and yet no 'formal' mention of Abyssinia occurred at the Stresa Conference in April 1935. Britain's silence, in Mussolini's view, implied consent.

But as the summer progressed, Britain made it clear that she would not approve of Italian annexation of the whole of Abyssinia. Britain's hostile reaction surprised and then angered Mussolini, but he determined to go through with his plan. Throughout the summer the world was presented with the spectacle of a crisis in slow motion. It was clear that Italy was planning a major invasion in the autumn when the rainy season ended. Attempts were made to reach a compromise settlement but with no success.

In June 1935 the Conservative leader, Stanley Baldwin, replaced MacDonald as Prime Minister. Sir Samuel Hoare became Foreign Secretary and Anthony Eden entered the Cabinet as Minister for League of Nations Affairs. Hoare had relatively little experience in foreign affairs and needed time to find his feet. This may have given civil servants like Sir Robert Vansittart more influence than usual. Vansittart considered Germany the main threat to Britain and in consequence was keen to appease Italy. On balance, however, the change of government made very little difference to British policy. Continued efforts were made to reach a compromise by offering Mussolini parts of Abyssinian territory. The Abyssinian Emperor, Haile Selassie, was prepared to accept some loss of land, but Mussolini was not satisfied with what he was offered. In October 1935 Italy invaded Abyssinia.

c) British Reaction to the Italian Invasion of Abyssinia

Haile Selassie immediately appealed to the League of Nations. Britain and France were now faced with a terrible choice. Haile Selassie was hardly a model ruler and Abyssinia was hardly a good neighbour. Abyssinia had caused Britain as much trouble on the Sudanese frontier as Italy had experienced on the Eritrean frontier. Britain, ironically, had unsuccessfully opposed Abyssinia's entry into the League of Nations in 1923. Neither Britain nor France had any real interests in Abyssinia. To take action, whether economic or military, against Mussolini would wreck the Stresa Front and, even worse, might force Italy into an agreement with Hitler.

But serious principles were at stake. The main one was whether Britain should honour her obligations under the League covenant. Public opinion in Britain was strongly opposed to the Italian invasion. The results of the so-called Peace Ballot, held in 1934 but not declared until June 1935, showed considerable popular support for the League. Over 11,500,000 people had voted in the ballot, held at the behest of the League of Nations Union; 95 per cent thought Britain should remain in the League and large majorities had voted in favour of supporting economic and, if necessary, military measures against aggressor states. Public opinion could not be ignored, if only because a general election was in the offing. Despite its previous readiness to consider concessions, the British government now took a moral stand. It condemned the Italian invasion and supported the League of Nations' action against Italy. The French government, anxious not to drive Mussolini into the German camp but equally anxious to keep in step with Britain, did likewise.

In October the League denounced Italy as the aggressor and imposed economic sanctions. All imports from Italy and some exports to her were banned by virtually all members of the League. 70 per cent of Italy's trade was with League members and it was assumed that economic pressure would bring Italy to a negotiated settlement.

In the same month Baldwin announced a general election. The National Government's sanctions policy – cheap, popular and avoiding war – was nicely tailored to the requirements of the election campaign. As far as foreign policy was concerned, both Labour and the National Government said much the same thing; both committed themselves to the principle of collective security and both talked in general terms of the benefits of disarmament. Baldwin, although promising to 'remedy the deficiencies which have occurred in our defences' refused to emphasise new rearmament plans for fear of losing support. With the economy improving and Baldwin inspiring calm, the National Government won a handsome victory, polling 11.8 million votes and winning 432 seats. Labour polled 8.3 million votes, winning 154 seats. The Liberals won 20 seats and the Communists one.

By early December most members of the League, headed by Britain and France, were applying a trade embargo against Italy. But the sanctions, which did not include an embargo on oil, did not seriously threaten the Italian war effort. If anything they simply unified the Italian people behind Mussolini. Closure of the Suez Canal might have been an even better way of damaging the Italian war effort than oil sanctions, but this might have led Mussolini to the 'mad dog act' of declaring war on Britain. The British government had no wish for a war against Italy, from which only Japan and Germany could benefit.

In December 1935 the British and French Foreign Ministers, Hoare and Laval, met in Paris to discuss the Abyssinian situation. They decided to propose a compromise settlement. Italy would receive about one third of Abyssinia; in return Haile Selassie would remain Emperor and would be ceded a strip of Italian territory, giving Abyssinia access to the Red Sea. The British Cabinet approved the plan and Mussolini was ready to agree to it. However, when details of the so-called Hoare-Laval Plan were leaked to the press, there was a storm of indignation, not least among Conservative MPs, who felt the government was breaking its election promises and betraying its commitment to the League. In the face of this outburst, the Cabinet decided to abandon the Hoare-Laval Plan.

Hoare took most of the blame and resigned. In his resignation speech he said he had no regrets and claimed that his policy offered the best solution that Abyssinia could now hope for. But Eden, the new Foreign Secretary, disliked and distrusted Mussolini and thought Britain should stand firm and support the League. In March 1936 Britain voted for oil sanctions but refused to impose a full scale naval blockade, and oil from the USA continued to flow into Italy. Nothing more was done to make sanctions bite.

d) The Situation by 1936

Meanwhile the Italians fought well. In May 1936 Haile Selassie fled and Abyssinia became part of the Italian Empire. Mussolini's prestige in Italy soared. He boasted that 'the greatest colonial war in all history was the foundation stone of a new Roman Empire'.

In June 1936 Neville Chamberlain described the continuation of sanctions as the 'very midsummer of madness'. A week later the sanctions were withdrawn. Chamberlain, like several other Cabinet members, had favoured a compromise solution throughout the crisis and was prepared to forgive Italian 'crimes' in the hope that Anglo-Italian friendship could be restored. But Britain continued to refuse to recognise the Italian conquest. This infuriated Mussolini and did Abyssinia little good.

The Abyssinian crisis had several important results. It was a death blow to the League of Nations, which had again failed to deter or halt an aggressor. This was a great shock to British public opinion. Collective security and the League, those concepts which had seemingly guarded British and world peace without the necessity to spend vast sums on armaments, had failed. The crisis had also caused a major split between Italy and Britain and France. Mussolini felt bitter at the way he had been treated by the western powers. Although he still regarded

Hitler with some suspicion, he began to move closer to the German dictator who had consistently supported Italy's actions in Abyssinia.

Some historians have accepted Churchill's view, that the failure to check Mussolini in 1935–6 was an important step on the way to world war. They argue that Britain and the League should have been prepared to fight Mussolini. The assumption is that Italy would have been easily defeated and that this would have strengthened collective security and helped to deter later German aggression. But recently this argument has been questioned. Almost certainly Britain would have won a war against Italy; but victory would have left an embittered Italy and might not have been as easy as many have assumed. Italy was reasonably well prepared for war in 1935–6 – unlike Britain. Moreover, Britain could scarcely have afforded the losses she was likely to sustain in even a successful war.

However, most historians are agreed that British policy in 1935–6 was weak and inept. It fell between two stools: the search for a compromise with Italy on the one hand; and the need to stand firm against Italian aggression on the other. In the end nothing had been achieved. Britain had failed to uphold collective security and to appease Mussolini. To make matters worse, the Abyssinian crisis had revealed serious divisions between Britain and France.

Hitler was not slow to appreciate this weakness and division. He was also able to use the Abyssinian crisis for his next great gamble.

5 The Rhineland, Spain and Rearmament

a) The Rhineland

In March 1936 Hitler sent German troops into the demilitarised Rhineland. By so doing, he was clearly violating both the Treaty of Versailles and the Treaty of Locarno, freely accepted by Germany in 1925. Hitler's excuse was the ratification by the French Senate of the 1935 Franco-Soviet alliance, which he claimed was a threat to Germany. Hitler knew he was taking a considerable gamble. Germany was not strong enough to fight a long war and the token German forces that marched into the Rhineland had orders to withdraw at the first sign of French opposition.

Neither the French nor British governments had been altogether surprised by Hitler's action. Both governments had expected that Hitler would raise the issue of the Rhineland as a topic for negotiation and both had a number of prior warnings about the German move from their intelligence staffs. Unlike the British, the French had the forces available to take action, but the unstable political situation in France made a French call to arms unlikely. In the event, the French caretaker government did nothing – except pass the problem to Britain by asking if she would support French action.

The British government made it clear that it had no intention of risking war against Germany. Most British opinion saw Hitler's move into the Rhineland as regrettable in manner but not particularly threatening in substance. Most MPs probably agreed with Lord Lothian's remark that Germany had every right to walk into its own 'backyard'. Some French politicians later claimed that France did not take action because Britain failed to offer support. However, it now seems certain that there was no will in France to risk war with or without British support.

Hitler had once again gambled and won. His troops remained in the Rhineland and began to build fortifications along the French frontier. Henceforward it would be even more difficult for Britain or France to take action against Germany.

In retrospect, many historians have claimed that Germany's march into the Rhineland was 'the last chance' to stop Hitler without war, and thus the point at which he could and should have been challenged. It is possible that the threat of force might have forced him to back down and that he might, in consequence, have suffered a disastrous blow to his prestige. However, it was far from clear to French leaders at the time that Hitler would have pulled out of the Rhineland – and some historians have questioned the long-held view that he would have retreated if France and Britain had stood firm. In 1936 Germany might not have been the easy push-over that many historians have assumed. Certainly there was little that Britain could have done immediately to help France.

Only a few British politicians, most notably Winston Churchill, pressed for a resolute stand against Germany. Most MPs thought that there was still insufficient evidence to suggest that Hitler's ambitions were entirely open-ended and violent. Anthony Eden, for example, believed that there might be much to be gained by accepting the German move and taking seriously Hitler's new proposals for a 25-year non-aggression pact. Through the summer of 1936 attempts were made to reach a stronger Anglo-German agreement. These attempts failed, but at least Britain and Germany remained on reasonably good terms throughout most of 1936–7. Hitler declared that he had no territorial claims in Europe, and for nearly two years he maintained a remarkably low profile. Germany continued to rearm – but not on the scale that many in the west later believed.

b) The Spanish Civil War

In July 1936 the attention of most British statesmen changed from Germany to Spain. Right-wing nationalists, led by General Franco and supported by monarchists, the Catholic Church and most of the armed forces, tried to overthrow the left-wing Republican Government. The Republican Government, supported by the industrial working class, liberals, socialists and communists, fought back.

British public opinion was excited and divided by the Spanish Civil War. The Labour Party and the left saw Franco as a fascist 'puppet' and strongly supported the Republicans. About 2000 people from Britain went to Spain to join the International Brigade and fight against Franco, convinced that they were waging war against fascism. However, others sympathised with the Nationalists, saw the Republicans as essentially communist-inspired, and some even went to fight on Franco's side.

The British government had little sympathy for either side in the civil war. Britain's main aim was to prevent the war spreading and becoming a general European conflict between the great powers. Therefore the government supported the setting up of a Non-Intervention Committee to discourage intervention on either side and enforce a ban on the export of war materials to Spain. Significantly the League of Nations was largely ignored! Most of the powers joined the Committee but it was soon clear that its decisions were being flouted by Italy, Germany and Russia.

Mussolini supplied aircraft, armaments and nearly 100,000 men to help the Nationalists. Italian submarines sank merchant ships suspected of trading with the Republicans. Germany sent far fewer men, but used the war to test the value of new weapons and military techniques. The destruction of the small town of Guernica by German bombers in April 1937 made a great impression on contemporaries. Russia soon sent men and weapons in an effort to help the communists on the Republican side. Spain, therefore, was transformed into the battleground of rival ideologies – the forces of communism against the forces of fascism.

The civil war dragged on for three bloody years. British fears that it might lead to a general war proved to be unfounded. Crises occurred, but in each case agreements were cobbled together. However, many people in Britain were convinced that should a general war occur, the line-up would be on ideological grounds, rather than on grounds of perceived 'national interest'. Many on the left thought Britain should align herself on the anti-fascist side. Many on the (Conservative) right, on the other hand, while having little time for fascism, had no wish to align themselves with socialists and communists. Conservative opinion, on the whole, thought it was in Britain's best interest to stay out of any future ideological conflict.

Germany probably benefitted most from the Spanish Civil War. Not only did the war give Hitler an opportunity to test his new weapons, but it led to improved relations with Italy. In November 1936 Mussolini proclaimed the Rome-Berlin Axis. In 1937 Italy joined Germany and Japan in the Anti-Comintern Pact. Relations between Britain and Italy sank to a new low.

c) Rearmament

By the end of 1936 Britain faced serious problems. Germany was rearming, Italy was a potential threat in the Mediterranean and Japan had a substantial navy in the Far East. The diplomatic outlook was not hopeful. The League system was bankrupt and Britain had few strong, reliable allies.

In the circumstances Britain seemed to have little alternative but to rearm. The National Government was still hesitant. Extra military spending meant sacrificing other, more popular, programmes – housing, health or education. But already in 1935 a Defence White Paper had concluded that, 'Additional expenditure on the armaments of the three Defence Services can no longer be postponed'. In 1936 a Minister for the Co-ordination of Defence was appointed. Churchill would have loved the job, but it was given to Sir Thomas Inskip, a lawyer with no previous experience of the armed forces. Lord Cherwell, one of Churchill's friends, remarked that Inskip's appointment was 'the most cynical thing that has been done since Caligula appointed his horse a consul'.

In 1936 Chamberlain introduced an extensive four-year plan for rearmament. This provided the framework for the military structure with which Britain entered the war in 1939. To help pay for it he placed a tax on tea, widely denounced as an attack on working class living standards. The increased rearmament was deplored by the Labour Party. The government, far from failing to rearm, was accused of rearming on 'a gigantic scale' and with too great haste. Most Labour MPs continued to oppose every major initiative for increased defence funding, right through to the introduction of conscription in 1939.

One of Britain's main problems was that she had to prepare for several different types of war. She had to be ready to fight a colonial war, a naval war in the Far East, and a great European war. The nightmare scenario was that she might have to fight all three potential enemies – Germany, Italy and Japan – at the same time. Priority was naturally given to those services which could defend Britain from attack. Naval strength was essential to defend vital trade routes. Air defences were also a major concern. Far less money was spent on the army. Building bombers was seen as a cheaper and better way of preventing war in Europe than spending vast sums on building a large army. Given the possibility of a long war of attrition, the government began to stockpile strategic materials and make detailed plans for economic mobilisation. Much of this important economic rearmament was hidden from the public.

More money could, and perhaps should, have been spent on rearmament, as Winston Churchill claimed at the time and later. But the Treasury advised caution. Treasury officials and military experts realised that economic strength was the fourth arm of defence, without

	BRITAIN	GERMANY	ITALY	JAPAN	WORLD
1931	National Government replaced Labour Government	Weimar Republic	Mussolini and Fascists in power	Liberal Politicians – challenged by army and radical Nationalists Manchuria	World-wide Depression
1932	Ottawa Conference Imperial protection	Lausanne Conference The end of reparations	Plans for Abyssinian invasion	Manchukuo set up Lytton Commission	Depression continues World Disarmament Conference
1933		Adolf Hitler came to power Germany left League of Nations and World Disarmament Conference		Japan left the League of Nations	
1934	Peace Ballot	Non-aggression pact with Poland	Stopped Nazi *putsch* in Austria		
1935	Baldwin replaced MacDonald as P M Hoare – Laval Pact	Re-introduced conscription Anglo - German Naval Agreement	Stresa Front Invasion of Abyssinia		Franco-Russian treaty League of Nations imposed sanctions on Italy
1936	4 year Rearmament Plan	Remilitarisation of Rhineland Rome – Berlin Axis	Abyssinia became part of Italian Empire	Anti-Comintern Pact with Germany	Spanish Civil War

Summary – The Gathering Storm 1931–6

which purely military efforts would be of no avail. Britain was short of machine tools and skilled labour. Up to one sixth of the 1937 arms programme had to be met from imports. Increased military spending meant running the risk of a serious balance of payments crisis or a run on the pound or both. This would undermine Britain's ability to continue importing for rearmament. Those, like Churchill, who argued in favour of more defence spending, ignored the constraints of Britain's industrial capacity. The gradual expansion of forces, which avoided the temptation to spend large sums of money on weapons which would soon be outdated, also made considerable sense.

Making Notes on 'The Gathering Storm 1931–6'

Your notes on this chapter should give you an understanding of the international problems that faced British governments between 1931 and 1936, particularly with regard to Germany, Italy and Japan. British foreign policy in the 1930s has often been criticised (most notably by Winston Churchill). As you read the chapter try to identify what Britain could have done that was different. Should Britain have taken stronger action against Hitler, Mussolini and Japan? Why did she fail to take action? It is important that you have a good understanding of why British statesmen acted as they did. You should also have opinions, supported by evidence, about whether they were wise or foolish to act as they did. To appease or not to appease is still an important issue in foreign affairs today.

Answering essay questions on 'The Gathering Storm 1931–6'

Examiners have proved themselves to be very resourceful in designing questions on this period and you must expect to be asked to tackle questions that group together aspects of the topic in a wide variety of ways:
a) Some questions cover all aspects of British foreign policy in the 1930s.
b) Some questions concentrate on one aspect, such as British relations with Germany.
c) Some questions focus on the wisdom or foolishness of British statesmen.
Many questions ask you to look at events before 1931 or after 1936. Consider the following:

1 Discuss the changing attitudes and policies of British governments towards Germany from 1919 to 1938.
2 In what ways did Britain's relations with Germany and Italy after 1933 contribute to the 'gathering storm' of international mistrust and hostility that was to lead to war in September 1939?
3 Can the handling of foreign policy by the British governments of 1931–9 be defended?

Pay particular attention to the timescales covered by each question. Question 1 requires you to include information from this chapter and chapters 1 and 2. Questions 2 and 3 require evidence from this chapter and chapters 5 and 6.

Question 1 is a relatively straightforward question and best done chronologically. You will need to go back to chapters 1 and 2 to discover Britain's attitude to Germany in 1919–33. Did Hitler's coming to power in Germany make any difference to British policy? Should it have made any difference? How did Britain respond to Hitler's pressure in the period 1933–6? The question does not specifically ask you to praise or criticise British responses, but you will lose no marks by passing comments and showing that you are aware of some of the main debates about British policy, especially in the 1930s! It is worth making a rough plan of the main paragraphs of the essay. From the point of view of your plan assume that the ending date is 1936 rather than 1938.

Source-based questions on 'The Gathering Storm 1931–6'

1 Germany withdraws from the Disarmament Conference and the League of Nations
Study the cartoon reproduced on page 77. This was drawn by Low in 1933. Answer the following questions:
a) What positions did Simon, Daladier and Mussolini hold and which countries did they represent? (**3 marks**)
b) Comment on Mussolini's position in the cartoon. (**3 marks**)
c) Comment on the representation of the League of Nations. (**3 marks**)
d) Comment on the way the cartoonist has represented Hitler. (**3 marks**)
e) To what extent, if any, does the cartoon display the political bias of the cartoonist? (**3 marks**)

2 The German Threat 1933–5
Read the speeches of Churchill, Simon and Baldwin on pages 76, 77 and 78. Answer the following questions:

a) According to the evidence in the extracts, how was Germany breaking the Treaty of Versailles in 1934? (**2 marks**)
b) On what points did Churchill and Simon agree? (**2 marks**)
c) On what points did Churchill and Baldwin agree? (**2 marks**)
d) Over what issues was Churchill critical of the government? (**3 marks**)
e) Given the German air threat, what possible courses of action might Britain have taken? Which action do you think would have been the best and why? (**6 marks**)

CHAPTER 5

Chamberlain and Appeasement 1937–8

1 Neville Chamberlain

a) Background

In May 1937 Stanley Baldwin retired. Neville Chamberlain succeeded him as Prime Minister. Chamberlain's family was steeped in politics. His father, Joseph Chamberlain, had been a leading late nineteenth century politician – a radical and then an imperialist. His half brother, Austen, had been British Foreign Secretary in the 1920s. Neville had come to political life late, becoming an MP in 1918 when he was nearly 50. He had made his name first as a social reformer and then as a competent Chancellor of the Exchequer who had helped to steer Britain through the depression and along the road to economic recovery.

Chamberlain was the obvious choice of Prime Minister. He had considerable experience in high office and was widely respected within the Conservative Party and in parliament. He was seen as practical and 'safe'. He was, perhaps, a difficult man to like: cold, aloof and imperious. But he was an easy man to respect: tough, efficient and conscientious. Even Winston Churchill was lavish in his praise when seconding his nomination for the Conservative Party leadership.

Few thought that the change of Prime Minister would mean dramatic changes of policy. Chamberlain belonged to the same party as Baldwin and the two men had cooperated closely on domestic and foreign issues. Both were patriots who were wedded to the idea of the British Empire. Both hated socialism. Baldwin supported, and in many ways had groomed, Chamberlain as his successor. Chamberlain reshuffled the Cabinet but his team was essentially the same as Baldwin's. Eden remained as Foreign Secretary.

However, there were to be differences. Baldwin had lacked dynamism and, after 1935, could be accused of allowing policy to drift. Chamberlain, though 68 years old (only two years younger than Baldwin), was determined to play a more vigorous and positive role. His style contrasted sharply with that of Baldwin. He was less concerned with consensus. He was also determined to control foreign policy and not be controlled by civil servants or by his Foreign Secretary. Although he took advice from an 'inner cabinet' of ministers and friends, many saw his leadership style as autocratic. His feeble appearance and bleating voice belied his confidence and strength of purpose.

b) Aims

The word now indissolubly linked to Chamberlain's name is 'appeasement'. For many years after the Second World War appeasement had a bad press. Those who had supported it were seen as the 'Guilty Men' whose misguided policies had helped to bring about war. The appeasers were portrayed as cynical defenders of the capitalist system who hoped to drive Germany and Russia into mutual destruction, or as timid cowards. Chamberlain was usually seen as Guilty Man Number 1.

However, many historians now view appeasement and Neville Chamberlain in a different and far more positive light. They point out that the main ideas of appeasement were not something that Chamberlain invented. For hundreds of years it has been a cardinal principle of British foreign policy that it is better to resolve international disputes through negotiation and compromise than through war. Some historians think that in the circumstances of 1937–8 Chamberlain had little alternative but to appease. Appeasement had its dangers, but so did all other possible courses of action. Even now it is difficult to see what realistic alternatives there were to appeasement – except war.

Chamberlain was certainly not an ignorant muddler in foreign affairs as some historians have suggested. He had been closely involved in all matters of government throughout the 1930s and, as Chancellor of the Exchequer, had been particularly good at noting the interconnections of foreign and financial policy.

It was evident to Chamberlain, as to everybody else, that soon there would be enormous changes in the relative international standing of the great powers – especially Germany. There was little Chamberlain could do about this. The main question was whether these changes could be effected without war and, if so, what role could Britain play. Chamberlain loathed the prospect of war which, in his view, 'wins nothing, cures nothing, ends nothing'. Consequently he was prepared to go to considerable lengths to preserve peace. However, he was not a pacifist. If Britain's vital interests (such as the preservation of Britain and its empire) were at stake he was prepared to fight. But he hoped he could ensure, by reason and concession, that those vital interests were not endangered.

Chamberlain believed that the maintenance of peace could not be achieved without British participation in European affairs. He thought that Britain, because of her geographical separation from Europe, might have a special position to play as conciliator and mediator. He had no illusions about how difficult a task he faced, but he believed that just settlement of many of the reasonable grievances of Germany, Italy and Japan was possible.

The new Prime Minister had no confidence in the League of Nations or in collective security. When President Roosevelt suggested a world conference to discuss world problems, Chamberlain considered the idea to be 'drivel'. He had been a businessman and liked the idea of face-to-face, business-like discussions between statesmen. The interested parties would then devise new contracts which they would thereafter make every effort to observe.

Chamberlain knew he could count on little support from Britain's potential allies. Throughout the 1930s France was ruled by a series of weak and short-lived governments and Chamberlain had no confidence in the country or its statesmen. He had even less confidence in the USSR. He feared and distrusted Stalin and communism as much as he feared and distrusted Hitler and Nazism.

Chamberlain hoped for more from the USA. He was aware that, without American assistance in the First World War, Britain and France might well have been defeated. But he was also aware that there was little prospect of American involvement in European or world affairs. In the 1930s the USA was overwhelmingly isolationist and had no wish for foreign entanglements. Most Americans believed they had been forced into entering the First World War by big bankers and manufacturers intent on making high profits. In the late 1930s the American Congress passed a series of Neutrality Acts preventing the USA from selling arms or giving loans to any country involved in war. These were designed to keep the USA out of any future wars.

President Roosevelt had some sympathy with Britain and France. In October 1937 he made his so-called 'quarantine' speech, calling for a concerted effort to oppose those countries who were creating 'a state of international anarchy'. However, such talk was not followed by action. Roosevelt, with a shrewd eye on American public opinion, held aloof from international commitments which might entangle the USA in foreign wars. The USA would not even join in a stand against Japanese aggression when American commercial and strategic interests were plainly threatened.

'It is always best and safest', thought Chamberlain, 'to count on nothing from the Americans but words'. However, aware of the importance of USA economic help to Britain in the First World War, he was reluctant to become involved in another European conflict without some assurances of American support. In addition, he was aware that Britain could not rely on the British Dominions, whose support had also been so important in the First World War. Canada and South Africa were reluctant to become involved in European problems, while Australia and New Zealand were concerned more with Japan than the threat from Germany or Italy.

Chamberlain has been criticised for lacking an insight into the minds of Hitler and Mussolini. However, few politicians then – and few historians since – successfully analysed the intentions of the dictators. Chamberlain did not trust Hitler, Mussolini or the Japanese. (He soon believed Germany to be the 'bully of Europe' and Hitler 'utterly untrustworthy and dishonest'.) For this reason he was not simply intent on appeasing the dictators. He also favoured rearmament. He was convinced that 'you should never menace unless you are in a position to carry out your threat'. Until Britain was adequately armed, 'we must adjust our foreign policy to our circumstances and even bear with patience and good humour actions which we would like to treat in a very different fashion'.

Chamberlain wrote in 1937, 'I believe the double policy of rearmament and better relations with Germany and Italy will carry us safely through the dangerous period, if only the Foreign Office will play up'. He was suspicious of the Foreign Office and claimed in private that it had 'no imagination and no courage'. He was quite prepared to use his own intermediaries and communicated directly, rather than through the Foreign Office, with some ambassadors, such as Sir Nevile Henderson in Berlin. Henderson pictured Hitler as a moderate with limited aims, a man with whom it was possible to do business. Henderson's despatches probably helped to confirm Chamberlain in his policies.

Although Chamberlain's personal diplomacy sometimes angered the Foreign Office, there seems little doubt that the policy he pursued was supported by the great majority of the Cabinet, MPs and the British public. Recent research has suggested that the government actively manipulated public opinion through a variety of propaganda techniques in order to sustain support for appeasement policies. However, this is far from proven. What is certain is that the vast majority of the British people were repelled by the prospect of war.

Winston Churchill was the most prominent anti-appeaser. He was later to acquire the reputation of having been right on Hitler, whereas Chamberlain had been wrong. But Churchill's views derived not from a prolonged study of Hitler, but from his own preconceptions and anti-German prejudices. There were not many in Britain who cared to go along with his hunches and prejudices in 1937–8. He had been wrong on too many occasions in the past. He was seen by many as a right-wing maverick and war-monger. Only a small, uncoordinated cluster of Conservative MPs supported his anti-appeasement line.

The Labour Party disliked Chamberlain and hated Hitler, Mussolini and fascism. Some Labour MPs objected to Chamberlain's policy to the dictators simply because it was Chamberlain's policy! But Labour proposed no real alternative, never mind consistent, course of action. Most Labour MPs opposed every initiative for increased defence spending. They preached a strong policy supported only by strong words.

Although British military intelligence exaggerated German military power, and particularly the damage the German Luftwaffe might do to Britain, there was no doubt that Nazi Germany was certain to be a difficult enemy to defeat in the event of war – a fact which Churchill and many Labour MPs failed to appreciate.

2 The Problem of Japan 1937–9

Chamberlain immediately faced problems in the Far East. In July 1937 Chinese-Japanese hostility escalated into full-scale war, destroying any possibility of Japan being reintegrated into the international community. The incident which led to an extension of the war was triggered by China not Japan. Even so Japanese forces quickly took over large areas of China and Japan proclaimed her intention of securing a new order in East Asia.

Chamberlain seemed to have little alternative but appeasement. He was faced with a worsening situation in Europe and could not risk a conflict with Japan. His government urged restraint and appealed for an end to the conflict, but in vain. Efforts to co-ordinate policy with the USA had only limited success. The USA showed no signs of wanting to play a decisive role in East Asia. In the circumstances the best British hope was that Japan would get bogged-down in a war of attrition in China – which indeed was what happened.

In the late 1930s British attention was focussed more on Europe than the Far East. However, Chamberlain could not avoid the fact that European and Far Eastern problems often interacted and that policy in each area was influenced by the other. Fear of Japanese aggression was an important factor in understanding why Britain was keen to conciliate Italy and Germany. The awareness that many Japanese leaders felt more at home with Nazi Germany and Fascist Italy than with Britain and the other western democracies was a further reason for caution.

3 Chamberlain's Initiatives in Europe, 1937–8

In July 1937 Chamberlain explained to the Cabinet the impossibility of fighting Germany, Italy and Japan at the same time. The only solution was to find a way of separating these powers by diplomatic means. He intended to explore the prospects of a settlement with each potential enemy in turn. His hope was to detach them from the aggressive bloc one by one by active examination of their grievances.

In the autumn of 1937 Chamberlain sent his friend Lord Halifax, an ex-Viceroy of India, to visit Hitler to find out precisely what Hitler wanted. (Eden was not altogether happy about the visit by a colleague who had no responsibility for foreign affairs!) Conversations between Halifax and the Nazis ranged widely. Halifax made it clear that Britain was prepared to accept some changes in Austria, Czechoslovakia and Poland, provided the changes came about through peaceful means. Britain was also ready to consider giving Germany some colonies in

Africa. (This was to be at the expense of Belgium and Portugal, rather than Britain or her Dominions.) Hitler had little interest in African colonies, but indicated that he still hoped for an agreement with Britain. He certainly seemed to pose no immediate threat. Indeed Germany had better relations with Britain than with any other western government. The two states were important trading partners and Britain continued to provide Germany with considerable economic assistance, including credit and vital raw materials.

In 1937 Chamberlain spent a great deal of time trying to improve relations with Italy. Intent on a 'new impetus', the Prime Minister by-passed Eden and the Foreign Office and sent a personal letter to Mussolini urging that Britain and Italy should make a serious effort to resolve their differences. Mussolini responded favourably, but the continuation of the Spanish Civil War made an Anglo-Italian accommodation difficult. In August 1937 a torpedo, believed to have been fired by an Italian submarine, narrowly missed a British destroyer off Spain. A major incident was only just averted. In January 1938 Chamberlain finally initiated Anglo-Italian talks, but the outcome was inconclusive. Mussolini wanted Italian domination of the Mediterranean and North Africa, which Britain was not prepared to concede.

Chamberlain's efforts to reach an agreement with Mussolini led to major discord between the Prime Minister and Anthony Eden. Eden felt that his authority as Foreign Secretary was being undermined by Chamberlain's unwarranted intervention. He was also critical of Chamberlain's conduct of policy. He thought the Prime Minister should have made more effort to reach agreement with the USA and he was critical of Chamberlain's attempts to appease Mussolini. In Eden's view, the Italian leader was 'the complete gangster whose pledged word means nothing'. In February 1938 Eden resigned. In a statement to the Commons, he said 'I do not believe that we can make progress in European appeasement . . . if we allow the impression to gain currency abroad that we yield to constant pressure'.

The Prime Minister appointed Lord Halifax in Eden's place. He also replaced the anti-German Sir Robert Vansittart with a permanent Under-Secretary of State of his own choosing – Sir Alec Cadogan. Chamberlain was now much more in control of foreign affairs with compliant personnel to assist him.

In April 1938 Britain and Italy finally reached agreement. Britain would recognise Italy's position in Abyssinia in return for Italy withdrawing troops from Spain. The agreement was not to come into force until the Spanish question was solved. Anglo-Italian relations improved somewhat – but that was all. Italy remained a potentially hostile power and Mussolini continued his military build up in the Mediterranean. However, by the spring of 1938 German actions in central Europe had assumed a far greater significance than Italian actions in the Mediterranean.

4 The Anschluss

The union of Germany and Austria had been specifically forbidden by the Treaty of Versailles. However, Hitler had long harboured ambitions to annex Austria (his homeland) to Germany. He was encouraged by the fact that many Austrians also favoured union with Germany and that the Austrian Nazi party had considerable support within Austria. Since 1934 the Austrian government had struggled to keep Austrian Nazis under control and German influence at bay. Until 1936 it had the support of Italy, but, as Hitler and Mussolini drew closer together, it became obvious that Austria could no longer rely on Italian help. Throughout 1937 the Austrian Nazis, aided by money and advice from Berlin, increased their influence. By 1938 Schuschnigg, the Austrian Chancellor, felt he was losing control of the situation. In February 1938 he visited Hitler at Berchtesgaden, the Fuhrer's home in Bavaria, hoping to persuade him to restrain the Austrian Nazis. The meeting was a mistake. Hitler threatened and bullied the Austrian leader and insisted he should include Nazis in his Cabinet. Schuschnigg, shocked by Hitler's aggressive tactics, agreed to his demands and Seyss-Inquart, the Austrian Nazi leader, became Minister of the Interior.

It seems that Hitler planned to do little more at this stage. However, Schuschnigg again precipitated events. In early March he announced that he intended to hold a plebiscite to enable the Austrian people to decide whether they wished to become a part of Germany. Hitler, fearing the vote might go against him, was outraged. He demanded the cancellation of the plebiscite, whipped-up opposition amongst the Austrian Nazis and threatened war. Schuschnigg, aware that he could expect little support from Italy, Britain or France, resigned. His successor, Seyss-Inquart, immediately invited Hitler to send troops into Austria to preserve order. The hastily assembled German forces were enthusiastically welcomed by the Austrians. Hitler, himself, returned in triumph to his homeland and declared the union (or Anschluss) of Austria and Germany. The Anschluss, approved by a massive majority in a plebiscite run by the Nazis, had been achieved without serious fighting and was clearly a great success for Hitler.

The British government had little warning of the crisis – not surprisingly, because Hitler had decided to act only at the last minute. Chamberlain was not opposed to the Anschluss as such, but the way it had happened. He recognised that 'Nothing could have arrested this action by Germany unless we and others with us had been prepared to use force to prevent it'. Britain was not prepared to use the limited force she possessed. France, with a large army but without a government throughout the Austrian crisis, did nothing but protest. Mussolini, who had protected Austria in 1934, did not even do this.

It was, in fact, hard to argue that a great crime had occurred when so many Austrians expressed their joy at joining the Third Reich. Perhaps the most important feature of the Anschluss was not that it had happened, but how it had happened. If one frontier could be changed in this way, why not others? Hitler's excuse for the Anschluss was that there were large numbers of people of German stock in Austria demanding union with Germany. The uncomfortable fact was that there were similar populations of German-speaking people in other countries – Poland, Lithuania, Switzerland and, above all, Czechoslovakia.

5 The Problem of Czechoslovakia

a) The Situation in Czechoslovakia

The Anschluss immediately focused international attention on Czechoslovakia, much of which was now surrounded by German territory. The creation of Czechoslovakia had been, in Winston Churchill's view in 1919, 'an affront to self-determination'. By the 1930s only about half of the 15,000,000 population of Czechoslovakia were Czechs. The country contained over 2,000,000 Slovaks, 750,000 Hungarians, 500,000 Ruthenian, and 100,000 Poles. However, the largest minority ethnic group within Czechoslovakia were some 3,250,000 Germans. Most of these occupied the Sudetenland, which had been part of Austria-Hungary until 1918. By 1938 many Sudeten Germans, claiming they were victimised by the Czechs, were demanding either greater 'home rule' or, preferably, union with Germany. They received encouragement and support from Germany, where the Nazi press launched increasingly bitter attacks on the Czech government.

President Benes, the Czechoslovakian head of state, opposed the Sudeten German demands. He realised that if all the various ethnic groups within the country were given independence or self-rule, there would be no viable Czech state left. He was therefore determined to stand firm against German pressure.

Most British politicians had some sympathy with Czechoslovakia. Despite its astonishing ethnic composition and the fact that it did not treat its ethnic minorities particularly well, Czechoslovakia had preserved a democratic constitution more successfully than most other European states. It could also claim that it treated its minorities a good deal better than did most of its neighbours. A few politicians, such as Churchill, thought Czechoslovakia worth fighting for. Chamberlain was not among that number. He had little confidence in Czechoslovakia, which he regarded as a 'highly artificial' creation, and had some sympathy for the Sudeten Germans. He was quite willing to see the Sudetenland handed over to Germany, provided this could be done by negotiation rather than by force.

b) Chamberlain's Policy

In March 1938 Chamberlain told the Commons that British vital
interests were not involved in Czechoslovakia. Britain had no treaty
obligation to defend the Czech state and was in no position to offer
serious military aid. In late March 1938 he wrote:

1 You have only to look at the map to see that nothing France or we
  could do could possibly save Czechoslovakia from being overrun
  by the Germans if they want to do it . . . I have therefore
  abandoned any idea of giving guarantees to Czechoslovakia or the
5 French in connection with her obligations to that country.

The Chiefs of Staff agreed. On 28 March 1938 they reported to the
Cabinet that:

1 We conclude that no pressure that we and our possible allies can
  bring to bear, either by sea, on land or in the air, could prevent
  Germany from invading and overrunning Bohemia and from
  inflicting a decisive defeat on the Czechoslovakian army. We
5 should then be faced with the necessity of undertaking a war
  against Germany for the purpose of restoring Czechoslovakia's
  lost integrity and this object would only be achieved by the defeat
  of Germany and as the outcome of a prolonged struggle. In the
  world situation today it seems to us . . . Italy and Japan would
10 seize the opportunity to further their own ends and that in
  consequence the problem we have to envisage is not that of a
  limited European war only, but of a World War. On this situation
  we reported as follows some four months ago: 'Without overlook-
  ing the assistance we should hope to obtain from France and
15 possibly other allies, we cannot foresee the times when our
  defence forces will be strong enough to safeguard our territory,
  trade and vital interests against Germany, Italy and Japan simultaneously'.

Chamberlain's main concern was not so much Czechoslovakia but
France. The French, unlike Britain, did have an alliance with Czechos-
lovakia. Chamberlain feared that if Germany invaded Czechoslovakia,
France might go to her aid. Britain might then be forced to help
France. A German defeat of France would tilt the European balance so
overwhelmingly against Britain that it could not be contemplated.
Unbeknown to Chamberlain, the French had no wish to be drawn into
war over Czechoslovakia. Their strategic view was similar to the
British. Czechoslovakia could not be defended; Germany was too
strong.

Daladier, the new French Premier, and Bonnet, his Foreign Minister, were frantically looking for ways to avoid France's obligations to Czechoslovakia. They would be delighted if Britain gave them an excuse.

Mutual mistrust made a strong stance by both Britain and France unlikely. It was not clear to Chamberlain what France intended to do if Czech independence was threatened. On the other hand, the French were not certain that Britain would support them if it came to war. To make matters worse, it was still not clear to either Britain or France precisely what German demands were. (The ironic thing is that in the early spring of 1938 Hitler seems to have had no immediate designs on Czechoslovakia!)

Convinced that the Sudeten issue could no longer be ignored, Chamberlain determined to get ahead of events. In late March 1938 he formulated his policy:

1 My idea at present is that we should again approach Hitler
  following up our Halifax-Henderson conversations and say something like this. '. . . It is no use crying over spilt milk and what we
  have to do now is to consider how we can restore the confidence
5 you have shattered. Everyone is thinking that you are going to
  repeat the Austrian coup in Czechoslovakia. I know you say you
  aren't, but nobody believes you. The best thing you can do is to
  tell us exactly what you want for your Sudeten Germans. If it is
  reasonable we will urge the Czechs to accept it and if they do you
10 must give us assurances that you will let them alone in future'.

The main aim of Chamberlain's policy was to extract from the Czech government concessions which would satisfy the Sudeten Germans before Hitler used force to impose a settlement. This policy had the full support of Lord Halifax, the Cabinet and the Foreign Office, and was British policy in the fullest sense.

c) Increased Tension

The flaw in Chamberlain's policy was that the Czech government was in no mood to make concessions. In May, after what proved to be false reports of German troop movements, the Czechs mobilised some of their reserves and prepared for war. Both Britain and France, fearing a German attack on Czechoslovakia, warned Hitler against making such a move. Hitler was outraged by the Czech mobilisation and by the fact that the western powers seemed to have won a diplomatic victory because he had stepped back from invasion – an invasion which he was not actually then planning! This May crisis seems to have been a critical factor in persuading him towards a military confrontation with Czechoslovakia. He told his chief officers. 'It is my unalterable decision to smash Czechoslovakia by military action in the near future.'

As the summer wore on, tension increased. The German press stepped up its campaign against Czechoslovakia. The Czech government stood firm. There was internal crisis in France; the franc was under pressure and there was political instability. Daladier and Bonnet were quite happy to allow Britain to undertake the major initiatives in an effort to preserve European peace. Whatever happened this would have the advantage of involving Britain in eastern Europe. It might also be a way by which France could escape from the responsibilities of its alliance with Czechoslovakia.

Chamberlain has been criticised for ignoring the possibility of talks with the USSR. Russia, like France, had an alliance with Czechoslovakia and might have been prepared to support the western powers against Hitler. However, Chamberlain distrusted Stalin, suspecting that the Russian leader hoped that Britain and France would fight Germany which would be very much in Russian interests. Russia, moreover, was in the midst of the great purges and there seemed little Stalin could or would do. Military experts had assured Chamberlain that the Russian army lacked the capacity for an offensive war.

In June Britain proposed that a neutral mediator be sent to Czechoslovakia to try to resolve the crisis. The Czech government finally agreed and in August a mission led by Lord Runciman, a veteran Liberal politician with little diplomatic experience, travelled to Czechoslovakia to meet the various parties. Unfortunately neither the Sudeten Germans nor the Czechs were prepared to compromise and Runciman's mission, which lasted until mid-September, achieved little.

By September Chamberlain was increasingly anxious. British intelligence reported that Germany was planning a war against Czechoslovakia in early autumn. In Britain there was suddenly an awareness that a crisis was brewing. The country was divided. Some thought that Britain should support Czechoslovakia, but many, like Chamberlain, favoured the idea of self-determination for the Sudeten Germans and thought that war must be averted at almost all costs. The Prime Minister was aware that almost all the dominions were hostile to the idea of fighting for Czechoslovakia and realised the danger of taking a divided country and a divided empire into war. In September he wrote:

1 Over and over again Canning lays it down that you should never menace unless you are in a position to carry out your threats, and although, if we were to fight, I should hope we should be able to give a good account of ourselves, we are certainly not in a position
5 in which our military advisers would feel happy . . . to begin hostilities if we were not forced to do so.

[Canning was an able and successful British Foreign Secretary in the early 19th century.]

Hitler kept up the pressure. This was the only way he was likely to get the Sudetenland, as it was inconceivable that Czechoslovakia would give up a large amount of its territory without German pressure. At the Nuremberg rally in September, he criticised the Czech government, demanded self-determination for the Sudeten Germans and assured them they would be neither defenceless nor abandoned. Hitler's speech aroused great passion in the Sudetenland and the Czech government quickly declared martial law. Several Germans were killed and thousands more fled to Germany with tales of brutal repression. It seemed that war between Germany and Czechoslovakia was imminent.

6 The Munich Conference

a) Plan Z

Chamberlain now determined to put into effect the so-called Plan Z. He would fly to Germany to meet Hitler face to face and ask him what his demands really were. This proposal, according to Chamberlain, was 'so unconventional and daring that it rather took Halifax's breath away'. In the 1930s British Prime Ministers tended to stay at home and certainly did not fly abroad. Some historians think Chamberlain's plan was foolhardy: it committed Britain to imposing a negotiated settlement upon the Czech government. However, Plan Z received 'unanimous and enthusiastic' approval from the Cabinet and even most Labour MPs thought it a statesman-like gesture.

Chamberlain wrote a brief note to Hitler, asking to meet him. Hitler agreed. He may have been flattered by Chamberlain's proposal; but, like Chamberlain, he may also have been uneasy at the course of events. No one could feel even moderately certain what would happen if war broke out.

On 15 September Chamberlain boarded an aircraft for the first time in his life and flew to meet Hitler at Berchtesgaden. The two leaders talked for three hours and reached a rough agreement. Chamberlain accepted Hitler's main demand that all the areas in Czechoslovakia in which Germans comprised over 50 per cent of the population should be handed over to Germany. In return Hitler agreed not to attack Czechoslovakia until Chamberlain had made some important consultations.

Chamberlain flew back to Britain and set about convincing his Cabinet, the French and finally the Czechs that Hitler's demands, if met, would produce a lasting peace. The Cabinet and the French were

The Czechoslovak Crisis, 1938

The 'honest broker' from London urges Czechoslovakia not to allow himself to be shot by the brutal German with the machine-gun, advising him instead to put his head into the noose marked 'capitulation'.

Izvestiya, *Moscow, 16 September 1938*

won over with comparative ease. The Czech government, on the other hand, was appalled at the situation. However, without French or British backing, the Czechs had little option but to accept the loss of the Sudetenland. At least Chamberlain agreed to guarantee the new (weakened) state of Czechoslovakia in the event of it being threatened in future by Germany.

b) Godesberg

On 22 September Chamberlain flew back to Germany to meet Hitler at Bad Godesberg on the Rhine, expecting that, 'I had only to discuss quietly with him the proposals that I had brought with me'. To Chamberlain's consternation, Hitler said the previous proposals were insufficient. The claims of Poland and Hungary to Czechoslovakian territory had to be met and, in addition, he demanded the right to occupy the Sudetenland by force no later than 1 October. It is hard to say why Hitler increased his demands. Did he wish to humiliate the western powers – and if so why? Or did he think that now Poland and Hungary were making demands, Czechoslovakia would fall apart and there would be even more pickings for Germany? He was certainly taking a considerable gamble – unless he really wanted a war.

Chamberlain, 'Mein Kampf'. Cartoon by David Low

Faced with this new German ultimatum, Chamberlain returned to London. He was still in favour of accepting Hitler's demands but realised that there was now likely to be considerable opposition to such a course. This expectation proved to be correct. Many of Chamberlain's Cabinet colleagues, angry at Hitler's bullying tactics, rejected the Godesberg proposals. Daladier also expressed doubts about the wisdom of giving in to Hitler's demands and said that France would honour its commitments to Czechoslovakia. Not surprisingly, Czechoslovakia stated that the new proposals were totally unacceptable. War suddenly seemed likely. Both Britain and France began to mobilise. Trenches, for air-raid precautions, were dug in London parks. A few anti-aircraft guns were brought out and 38 million gas masks were distributed.

In what seemed like a last bid for peace, Chamberlain sent his personal envoy, Horace Wilson, to talk to Hitler. Wilson's mission failed. However, there was still one final hope. On 27 September the British Ambassador in Italy asked Mussolini to use his influence to persuade Hitler to reconsider. Mussolini agreed – but for a few hours it was uncertain whether his request to Hitler would have any effect. That same evening, Chamberlain broadcast to the British people:

1 How horrible, fantastic, incredible, it is that we should be digging
   trenches and trying on gas masks here because of a quarrel in a far
   away country between people of whom we know nothing . . . I
   would not hestitate to pay even a third visit to Germany, if I
5 thought it would do any good.

c) Munich

The next day, Chamberlain got his opportunity. He was speaking in the House of Commons, which had been recalled from holiday because of the crisis, when news came through that Hitler had accepted Mussolini's suggestion of a Four-Power Conference to be held at Munich to work out an agreement to the Sudeten question. The Commons erupted. Speeches of congratulation came from every side: everyone wanted to shake Chamberlain's hand. Attlee, the Labour leader, and Sinclair, the Liberal leader, blessed Chamberlain's mission. The prospect of an immediate war seemed to have been averted and it looked as though Hitler had backed down. Only Gallagher, the single Communist MP, spoke against Chamberlain going to the Munich Conference.

On 29 September Chamberlain, Daladier, Hitler and Mussolini met at Munich to discuss the fate of Czechoslovakia. Benes, the Czech leader, was not invited to the Conference. Nor was Stalin. The 12 hours of talks were remarkably casual and uncoordinated, but agreement was finally reached in the early hours of the 30 September.

The Munich agreement was very similar to Hitler's Godesberg

proposals, although it did water down some of Germany's most extreme demands. The Sudeten Germans were given self-determination within Germany. German occupation of the Sudetenland was to be carried out in five stages, spread out over ten days, rather than one. The precise borders of the new Czech state would be determined by a conference of the four Powers. Benes had no choice but to accept the Munich terms or fight alone. He chose to surrender.

Before returning to London, Chamberlain met Hitler personally and persuaded him to sign a joint declaration:

1   We regard the agreement signed last night and the Anglo-German Naval Agreement as symbolic of the desire of our two peoples never to go to war with one another again. We are resolved that the method of consultation shall be the method adopted to deal
5   with any other questions that may concern our two countries and we are determined to continue our efforts to remove every possible source of difference, and thus to contribute to assure the peace of Europe.

7 Munich: Success or Failure?

The Munich agreement, and Chamberlain's role in the whole Czechoslovakian crisis, have been the subject of massive debate ever since. The Munich Conference is usually viewed as a terrible failure for Britain. Many historians think that Chamberlain was outplayed by Hitler at almost every point. Britain had been humiliated and forced to sacrifice a friend to avert war. Czechoslovakia had been stripped of territory, so much so that she was now indefensible. Many think that Britain should have done the honourable thing and gone to war against Germany in 1938 rather than 1939.

However, Chamberlain saw Munich as a victory rather than a defeat. Hitler had backed down and not gone to war. Chamberlain thought Hitler had 'missed the bus'. In the Prime Minister's view, German military superiority over the western powers would never again be so great. He could claim that from a position of military weakness he had achieved most of his aims. He had avoided war, Germany's legitimate grievances had been settled, and Czechoslovakia had been kept in existence as a sovereign state.

In 1938 most people in Britain and France also thought of Munich as a triumph rather than a defeat. Both Chamberlain and Daladier were treated as heroes on their return from the Conference. Chamberlain was overcome by the large crowd which greeted him at the airport. He waved the piece of paper he had signed with Hitler and promised, 'Peace for our time'. Later, on the balcony at 10 Downing Street, he announced to cheering crowds, 'This is the second time in our History that there has come back from Germany to Downing Street peace with honour. I believe it is peace for our time.' President Roosevelt sent Chamberlain a telegram with the simple words: 'Good man'. Neville Henderson, the British Ambassador in Berlin, wrote a similarly congratulatory note – but with a degree of insight – 'Millions of mothers will be blessing your name tonight for having saved their sons from the horrors of war. Oceans of ink will flow hereafter in criticism of your action.'

The possible outcome of a war over Czechoslovakia in 1938 has intrigued historians ever since Munich. Many have accepted Churchill's view that it would have been better for Britain to fight Germany in 1938 than in 1939. Certainly Germany was not as strong in 1938 as Chamberlain and most British military experts imagined. She was short of tanks, fuel, ammunition, trained officers and reserves. Most German diplomats and generals were worried by the prospect of war. The Luftwaffe was not ready or able to launch a serious attack on Britain. The French army was still the best in Europe and Czech forces were far from negligible. The Czechs had a strong defence line along the German frontier and Russia might well have joined the war on Czechoslovakia's side.

However, it is far from certain that Britain and France would have been successful in 1938. In 1938 Britain was virtually defenceless against air attack. She had few fighter aircraft and very little radar defence. Neither country was ready for war. Czech armed forces were weak and divided; most Sudeten Germans and Slovaks prefered to fight against the Czechs than for them. Czech border defences were situated in the Sudetenland and were by no means complete. The Germans anticipated over-running Czechoslovakia in little more than ten days. French forces, deployed along the Maginot line, could have done little to help. It is far from certain that Russia would have come to Czechoslovakia's assistance. Neither Poland nor Rumania were prepared to tolerate Russian troops in their territory, so it would have been difficult for Russia to have sent direct help. Britain might also have lacked the support of several of her dominions and the British public was far from united in its determination to fight. It can thus be claimed (although this was not Chamberlain's intention) that Munich brought valuable time for Britain.

Interestingly, Hitler did not view Munich as a great triumph. Although he had gained the Sudetenland in return for nothing save a promise of future good conduct, he had been denied a military triumph. He was confident that he could have defeated Czechoslovakia quickly and regretted his decision to reach agreement at Munich.

8 The Aftermath of Munich

Chamberlain was not convinced that Munich made peace more secure. By now he seems to have had few illusions about Hitler and feared that

'A Great Mediator'. A Punch *cartoon, 1938*
John Bull: 'I've known many Prime Ministers in my time, sir, but never one who worked so hard for security in the face of such terrible odds.'

he would not be content with his recent gains. In private he regretted using the terms 'peace with honour' and 'peace for our time' in the euphoria of his return from Germany. However, he remained confident that he, and perhaps he alone, could handle the difficult problems that undoubtedly lay ahead. At least Munich gave him a breathing space. He would continue to hope and work for peace. With the Czechoslovakian problem out of the way, it might be possible to make further progress 'along the road to sanity'.

Some MPs were critical of the Munich agreement. Winston Churchill described the whole conduct of British policy as a 'total and unmitigated disaster'. Labour leaders censured Chamberlain for failing to obtain better terms, although no-one suggested what better terms might have been obtained.

Many Conservatives were uneasy that Hitler's bully-boy tactics seemed to have worked. But in the event only Duff Cooper, First Lord of the Admiralty, resigned, and less than 30 Conservatives abstained rather than support the motion by which the House approved the policy whereby war had been averted and peace was being sought.

The press was far from unanimous in support of Munich. *The Daily Worker*, *Reynolds News*, the *Manchester Guardian* and the *Daily Herald* were critical. Even the 'conservative' *Daily Telegraph* had reservations. But the majority of newspapers, both national and local, supported Chamberlain's policy and actions.

It is difficult to tell how the majority of people in Britain viewed the Munich agreement. Chamberlain certainly suffered no run of by-election disasters after September 1938. There was undoubtedly great relief that war had been averted and many gave Chamberlain credit for the preservation of peace. However, most Britons seem to have distrusted Hitler and to have feared for the future.

Public opinion polls, still in their infancy at this time, do seem to indicate an anti-German swing from October 1938 onwards. Here are some poll results from 1938–9:

Hitler says he has 'No more territorial ambitions in Europe'. Do you believe him? (Oct 1938)
  Yes 7%
  No 93%

In the present situation do you favour increases expenditure on armaments? (Oct 1938)
  Yes 72%
  No 18%
No opinion 10%

Which of these statements comes nearest to representing your

views of Mr Chamberlain's policy of appeasement? (Feb 1939)
1 It is a policy which will ultimately lead to enduring peace in
Europe – 28%
2 It will keep us out of war until we have time to rearm – 46%
3 It is bringing war nearer by whetting the appetite of the
dictators – 24%

In the autumn of 1938 Chamberlain's main concern was not opposition at home, but whether Hitler would abide by the terms and spirit of
the Munich agreement. He continued to work for improved relations
with Germany. Britain still held out the prospect of a return of some
German colonies and there were Anglo-German talks on industrial,
financial and trade links. The British government also welcomed and
encouraged an improvement in relations between France and Germany.
In December 1938 Ribbentrop, the German Foreign Minister, visited
Paris and signed a Franco-German agreement expressing mutual
goodwill and respect for frontiers.

Chamberlain also worked hard to improve relations with Italy. In
November he proposed the implementation of the Anglo-Italian agree-
ment of April 1938. While his critics questioned the extent to which the
previously stated British conditions had been satisfied, his action had
the overwhelming support of the House of Commons. In January 1939
Chamberlain and Lord Halifax visited Italy and met Mussolini.
Mussolini welcomed them but was not impressed. 'These are the tired
sons of a long line of rich men and they will lose their empire', he said.
But Chamberlain was pleased with the reception he received from the
Italian crowds and thought there was a good chance of detaching
Mussolini from Hitler.

In public Chamberlain and members of his government continued to
talk hopefully of Hitler and Mussolini's peaceful intentions. Their aim
was to avoid any increase in tension. However, the actions of Hitler in
particular gave little cause for optimism. The German leader refused to
make even the smallest sign of goodwill to Britain. Instead he made a
number of anti-British speeches and the German press continued to
make venomous attacks on its neighbour across the North Sea. Events
in Germany on the night of 9–10 November 1938 further damaged
Anglo-German relations. Following the killing by a Jew of a German
diplomat in Paris, Jewish shops throughout Germany were wrecked
and synagogues set on fire. 'Crystal Night' – as the Nazi anti-Jewish
pogrom became known – appalled most British people and destroyed
any remaining goodwill for Germany in Britain.

Making notes on 'Chamberlain and Appeasement 1937–8'

When making your notes on this chapter (and the next) you should
have three questions in your mind throughout. These are: i) What were

Chamberlain's aims in foreign policy? ii) Were these aims rational? (what alternative aims could he have adopted?) iii) How successful was Chamberlain in achieving his aims?

Unless you are a very experienced note-maker, you are unlikely to be able to organise what you write under these headings. You may be better advised to make your notes following the structure of the chapter, and to draw out your answers to the three questions afterwards. It is important to remember that your reading about Neville Chamberlain has not yet been completed. You should not reach any firm conclusions until you have read chapter 6.

Source-based questions on 'Chamberlain and Appeasement 1937–8'

1 The Czechoslovakian Crisis 1938
Read Chamberlain's and the Chiefs of Staff's views on the Czechoslovakian situation on pages 100 and 101. Answer the following questions:
a) To what extent do the views of Chamberlain and his Chiefs of Staff agree? **(3 marks)**
b) What were the Chiefs of Staff's main arguments against going to war over Czechoslovakia in 1938? **(2 marks)**
c) Explain the reference to the Halifax-Henderson conversations. **(4 marks)**
d) What precisely had Hitler done that had 'shattered' confidence? **(2 marks)**
e) Explain the main points of policy that Chamberlain was advocating in the extract on page 101. **(4 marks)**

2 The Munich Conference
Examine the three cartoons and read the extract from Chamberlain's broadcast to the British people on page 106 and the joint declaration signed with Hitler on page 107. Answer the following questions:
a) How far is the Russian cartoon a fair representation of what was happening to Czechoslovakia in 1938? **(4 marks)**
b) Comment on Chamberlain's point that this was 'a quarrel in a far away country between people of whom we know nothing'. **(3 marks)**
c) What evidence in the Punch cartoon bears out a point that Chamberlain made in his radio speech? **(2 marks)**
d) Contrast the different images of Chamberlain presented in the Punch and Low cartoons. **(6 marks)**
e) Why did Chamberlain regard the joint declaration as so important and was he right to do so? **(5 marks)**

3 British Opinions about Hitler
Examine the results of public opinion polls in Britain given on pages 110–11. Answer the following questions:

a) What information would a historian really need to know before assessing the value of these opinion polls as useful sources? (**4 marks**)
b) Assuming the polls do reasonably reflect public opinion, what are the most likely reasons why the October 1938 results as a whole seem to indicate an anti-German feeling in Britain? (**2 marks**)
c) To what extent does the February 1939 poll indicate support for Chamberlain's policy of appeasement? (**4 marks**)
d) What other evidence, apart from opinion polls, might give some indication of the views of the majority of the British people in 1938–9? (**5 marks**)

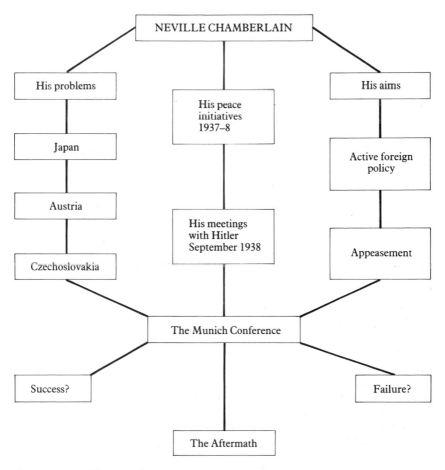

Summary – Chamberlain and Appeasement 1937–8

CHAPTER 6

The Coming of War, 1939

1 The Uneasy Peace, January–March 1939

In early 1939 Chamberlain received a number of disturbing (and incorrect) reports from British intelligence services predicting German moves against Poland, Czechoslovakia, the Ukraine, and even Holland or Switzerland. In February the Cabinet agreed that a German attack on Holland or Switzerland would lead to a British declaration of war. Lord Halifax, who was beginning to emerge as a political force in his own right, thought definite and clear limits should be placed on Germany's ambitions. His thinking was not very different from Chamberlain's. Neither man was prepared to give Hitler a totally free hand.

In the circumstances, Britain drew even closer to France. Both countries had common commitments to democracy and common fears about their own security. However, Anglo-French relations had been marked by years of mistrust. French politicians believed Britain might well leave them in the lurch and thought the British were not prepared to repeat the great 'effort of blood' made in the First World War.

Many British politicians, in return, were suspicious of the French. Chamberlain thought that France 'never can keep a secret for more than half an hour – nor a government for more than nine months'. As late as November 1938 the British Chiefs of Staff were opposed to conducting talks with France in too much detail for fear of being committed to a French war plan over which they had no control. In addition there were fears in London that France might be losing the will to resist Germany. Some French politicians seemed prepared to accept German predominance in eastern Europe. However, most were not. In 1938 pacifism had been the prevailing mood in France; but in 1939 the public mood swung in favour of resisting Nazi expansion. Most Frenchmen feared that if Germany gobbled up more territory in the east, she might ultimately prove too strong in the west.

The French government was anxious to obtain firmer pledges of British support. In particular it wanted Britain to commit itself to sending a large army to defend France. In February Chamberlain accepted that in the event of war Britain would have to help France defend its territory. He agreed to open detailed staff talks with the French. Britain also committed itself to raising an army of 32 divisions. This was a radical change in Britain's defence policy. Commitment to sending a large army to fight on the Continent, avoided for 20 years, was accepted.

Chamberlain, unlike many of his critics on the political left, had favoured British rearmament. After Munich he was more determined than ever that the pace of rearmament should not slacken. The best policy, he thought, was 'to hope for the best but be prepared for the worst'. In his view the main purpose of rearmament was to deter Hitler. Much of the increase in the number of aircraft in 1938–9 came from the maturing of plans which had been made in 1935. British rearmament had long been geared to reach its peak in 1939–40. But Britain's spending on rearmament rose considerably after October 1938. The production of aircraft increased from 240 a month in 1938 to 660 a month in September 1939. By the end of 1939 British aircraft production was expected to – and indeed did – overtake German production. This was partly because of increased emphasis on building fast fighter aircraft (Hurricanes and Spitfires) which were only a quarter of the cost of heavy bombers. Britain's radar defences improved considerably. In September 1938 only the Thames estuary had radar. By September 1939, a radar chain ran from the Orkneys to the Isle of Wight. There was suddenly the real possibility that the bomber would not always get through. Nevertheless in November 1938 Sir John Anderson was brought into the Cabinet and put in charge of air raid precautions. Plans were made for the evacuation of children from large cities in the event of war. Gas masks were distributed to everyone. Air raid shelters were dug and air raid officials were recruited and trained.

From 1936 to 1938 British intelligence had consistently exaggerated Germany's potential strength. However, after Munich it arrived at a more realistic assessment. It seemed that Germany, like Italy, faced a growing economic crisis and would not be able to risk, let alone sustain, a major war. In a long war of attrition, Britain and France's economic strength and the power of the naval blockade should ensure eventual victory. By 1939, therefore, Chamberlain was much more confident of Britain's capacity to fight, and in particular to resist air attack. As a result, he may have been prepared to take a firmer line than in 1938. But he still hoped for, and talked of, peace. In early March 1939, he predicted that Europe was 'settling down to a period of tranquility'.

2 The End of Czechoslovakia

Without its defences in the Sudetenland, Czechoslovakia was at Germany's mercy. It also faced serious internal problems. Many Slovaks had little love for what they saw as a Czech-dominated state. After Munich, Hitler deliberately encouraged the Slovaks to seek independence from Czechoslovakia. To make matters worse, Poland and Hungary continued to lay claim to Czechoslovakian territory. By early March the situation was so bad, internally and externally, that President Hacha, who had replaced President Benes, proclaimed martial law. This desperate attempt to preserve the unity of Czechoslovakia actually speeded its downfall. Hitler instructed the Slovak

nationalist leaders to appeal to Germany for protection and to declare
independence from Czechoslovakia. At the same time Hungary issued
an ultimatum demanding Ruthenia.

With his country falling apart, President Hacha asked for a meeting
with Hitler, hoping the German leader might do something to help
Czechoslovakia. Hitler received Hacha in the small hours of 15 March.
He told him that the German army intended to enter the country in a
few hours time and that his only choice was war or a peaceable
occupation. Hacha broke down under the threats and seems to have
suffered a minor heart attack. He recovered and signed a paper
entrusting the fate of the Czech people to Hitler. On 15 March, German
troops entered Czechoslovakia on the pretext that it was on the verge of
civil war. Hitler established a German protectorate of Bohemia and

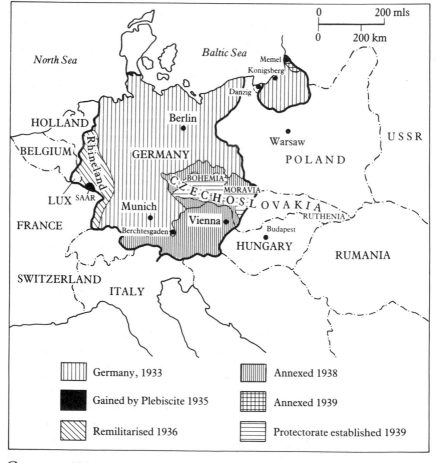

Germany, 1933 – August 1939

Moravia. Slovakia was nominally independent, but under German protection. Hitler allowed Hungary to take Ruthenia.

Hitler's take-over of Czechoslovakia had important repercussions. He had clearly ignored the Munich agreement, broken a signed agreement with Chamberlain and dismembered a small neighbour without warning or provocation. Moreover, this time he could not claim that he was uniting Germans within one German state. There was a sense of outrage in Britain as a whole and a marked shift of opinion in the Conservative Party and in the press. Most British people now felt that something must be done to stop Hitler before he controlled the whole of Europe.

Chamberlain's immediate pronouncement in the House of Commons was mild. He made it clear that there was no question of going to war. Czechoslovakia had collapsed as a result of internal disruption which freed the British government from any obligation. His apparent 'soft' line angered many MPs, and he faced pressure from the press, the Conservative Party, the Foreign Office and even from within his own Cabinet to do or say something stronger. All this clearly had an effect on Chamberlain. He would certainly have had political problems if he had continued meekly to accept Hitler's latest action. However, arguably he did not simply cave in to public pressure. He was indignant himself at the turn of events and Hitler's total disregard of the Munich agreement. His anger and determination to resist further German aggression was made clear at a speech he made at Birmingham on 17 March, the day before his seventieth birthday:

1 Germany under her present regime has sprung a series of unpleasant surprises upon the world. The Rhineland, the Austrian Anschluss, the severance of the Sudetenland – all these things shocked and affronted public opinion throughout the
5 world. Yet, however much we might take exception to the methods which were adopted in each of these cases, there was something to be said, whether on account of racial affinity or of just claims too long resisted, for the necessity of a change in the existing situation.
10   But the events which have taken place this week in complete disregard of the principles laid down by the German government itself seem to fall into a different category, and they must cause us all to be asking ourselves: 'Is this the end of an old adventure, or is it the beginning of a new? Is this the last attack upon a small
15 state, or is it to be followed by others? Is this in fact, a step in the direction of an attempt to dominate the world by force? It is only six weeks ago that . . . I alluded to rumours and suspicions which I said ought to be swept away. I pointed out that any demand to dominate the world by force was one which the democracies must
20 resist, and I added that I could not believe that such a challenge

was intended because no government with the interests of its own people at heart could expose them for such a claim to the horrors of world war.

And indeed, with the lessons of history for all to read, it seems
25 incredible that we should see such a challenge. I feel bound to repeat that, while I am not prepared to engage this country by new unspecified commitments, yet no greater mistake could be made than to suppose that, because it believes war to be a senseless and cruel thing, this nation has so lost its fibre that it
30 will not take part to the utmost of its power in resisting such a challenge if it ever were made.

The next day the British and French governments delivered sharp protests to Germany. Chamberlain told the Cabinet that his hopes of working with Hitler were over: 'No reliance could be placed on any of the assurances given by the Nazi leaders'.

3 The Polish Guarantee

a) German-Polish Relations

On 17 March there was a rumour that Germany was about to deliver an ultimatum to Rumania. The effects of this – totally false – rumour on the Foreign Office were electric. On 20 March Chamberlain proposed that Britain, France, Poland and Russia should issue a joint declaration that if there was a threat to the independence of any European state they would consult immediately on the steps to be taken. The British plan came to nothing. Poland had no wish to make any agreement with Russia. Stalin was also reluctant to commit himself.

Hitler may not have had immediate ambitions in Rumania, but he clearly had ambitions in eastern Europe. He now issued an ultimatum demanding that Memel, a town given to Lithuania after 1919, should be handed back to Germany. On 21 March Lithuania returned Memel. Britain and France took no action. It was inconceivable to think of going to war over Memel, a German city to which Hitler could lay reasonable claim. However, Poland now seemed to be Hitler's next target – and this was another matter.

There were some 800,000 Germans in Poland. The so-called Polish Corridor divided East Prussia from the rest of Germany (see the map on page 8). Danzig was 96 per cent German, and, although nominally a Free City under the supervision of the League of Nations, had been run by the Nazis since 1934. However Poland controlled Danzig's trade and foreign relations. This was a complicated and unsatisfactory arrangement, liable to create friction even with goodwill on all sides. No German government, whatever its political complexion, was likely to accept the Danzig solution as permanent, and Hitler's government was no exception. Polish governments were equally determined that things should remain as they were. The loss of Danzig to Germany might well compromise the rest of the gains Poland had made from Germany in 1919.

German relations with Poland had been remarkably friendly since the signing of the German-Polish non-aggression treaty in 1934. On a number of occasions, Germany had suggested to the Poles that the agreement might be turned into an alliance against Russia, but the Poles did not take up these suggestions. Polish foreign policy was chiefly concerned with avoiding any commitment either to Germany or to Russia which might involve Poland in future conflict.

After Munich, Hitler assumed that Poland would be drawn into the German orbit. In October 1938 Ribbentrop asked the Poles to give up Danzig. In return Poland would receive guarantees of her borders, German friendship and the prospect of territory in the Ukraine. In January 1939 Hitler met Colonel Beck, the Polish Foreign Minister, and added a demand for a German-controlled road or rail link across the Polish Corridor between East Prussia and the rest of Germany. To Hitler's surprise, the Poles refused to consider these relatively moderate suggestions. The Polish government was not willing to accept the status of a German satellite for its country. German demands became more insistent and uncompromising, but as yet there were no threats. In secret Hitler admitted that he was not simply after Danzig. The whole question of living space in the east was at stake. He needed Polish economic and labour resources. He was quite prepared to compel Poland, by force if necessary, to come within the German sphere. However, at this stage he hoped for a diplomatic rather than a military triumph. He did not want or expect a general European war.

However, tension mounted. The Polish government rejected the German proposals on Danzig and the Corridor and declared that any German attempt to alter the status of Danzig would lead to war. By the end of March there were rumours that a German attack on Poland was imminent. Britain and France feared that Poland might be overrun or forced to make terms with Germany unless they came to her support.

b) The Guarantee: Wise or Foolish?

On 31 March Britain took the unprecedented step of offering a guarantee to Poland: if she were the victim of an unprovoked attack, Britain would come to her aid. The French government offered a similar guarantee. The Polish government, still in secret negotiations with Germany over Danzig, accepted the British and French offers.

The Polish guarantee was widely condemned at the time and has been even more widely condemned since. Of all the east European states, Poland, a right-wing military dictatorship and very anti-semitic, was probably the one that Britain liked least. In fact, until 1939 Poland had few friends – except Germany! Poland had distanced herself from the League of Nations, had accepted Japanese and Italian expansion, and had won territory from Czechoslovakia in 1938–9. Beck, the Polish Foreign Minister, was considered totally untrustworthy. Hitler's demands of Poland – Danzig and access across the Polish Corridor – were far more reasonable than his demands of Czechoslovakia in 1938. Many historians regard the guarantees as 'blank cheques' given to a country notorious for its reckless diplomacy. Moreover, in the last resort, the 'cheques' were worthless because there was little that that Britain or France could do to support Poland! In the event of war France intended to defend the Maginot line, not attack Germany. Britain had no large-scale continental army and no plans to bomb German cities, because to do so would simply invite German retaliation.

However, and in defence of Chamberlain's 'U-turn' in policy, there was a feeling in political circles in Britain that something had to be seen to be done for foreign and domestic reasons. The Polish guarantee was designed as a clear warning to Hitler. If he continued to push for German expansion, he would face the prospect of a two-front war. Poland was seen as a useful ally, possibly stronger than the USSR, whom she had defeated in war in 1920–1, and certainly more reliable. Moreover, Chamberlain did not see the guarantee as a total commitment to Poland. There was a let-out clause. Britain had guaranteed Polish independence, not its territorial integrity. The guarantee did not mean that Poland might not be required to make certain territorial concessions. The future of Danzig was still thought to be negotiable. In Chamberlain's mind it was still a question of discovering the right mix of diplomacy and strength to persuade Hitler to negotiate honestly and constructively. The guarantee was intended to display British resolve and to deter Hitler from further aggression.

Unfortunately the guarantee angered, rather than deterred Hitler. He abandoned any thought of accommodation with Poland. At the end of March 1939 he ordered his Chief of Staff to prepare for war with Poland by the end of August. He was far from convinced that Britain and France would go to war to defend Poland.

4 The Drift to War

a) Mussolini's Actions

Mussolini was almost as disturbed as Chamberlain by the German occupation of Czechoslovakia. Hitler had left him ignorant of his intentions and this was a blow to the pride of the Italian dictator. Determined not to be outdone by Hitler, Mussolini embarked on his own foreign policy initiative. In April 1939 Italian forces occupied Albania, an Italian satellite in all but name since 1936. He also announced that the Balkans and the eastern Mediterranean should be

AN OLD STORY RETOLD

Herr Hitler. "It's all right; you know the proverb—'Barking dogs don't bite'?"
Signor Mussolini. "Oh, yes, *I* know it, and *you* know it; but does the dog know it?"

A cartoon from Punch, *5 April 1939*

regarded as being within the Italian sphere of influence.

This was a definite breach of the 1938 Anglo-Italian agreement. However, Britain had no wish to drive Mussolini into complete co-operation with Hitler. Chamberlain hoped that the Italian leader might exert a restraining influence on his German counterpart. Nevertheless Mussolini's aggressive words and actions, coming only three weeks after the take-over of Czechoslovakia and two weeks after Memel, seemed to indicate a greater degree of cooperation between Germany and Italy than was actually the case and to pose a further threat to east European stability. Britain and France now issued public guarantees to Greece and Rumania in the same terms as those given to Poland. In little more than two weeks Britain and France had undertaken obligations stretching from the Baltic to the Mediterranean.

Hitler was pleased by Mussolini's action. Italy's Balkan ambitions might well pre-occupy Britain and France while he settled the Polish question. It was a further bonus when Mussolini, to Hitler's surprise, proposed a close military alliance, which was signed in May in Berlin. The so-called 'Pact of Steel' required each power to help the other unconditionally in the event of war. This closer Italian-German friendship seemed to indicate there was little hope of detaching Mussolini from Hitler as part of the strategy for containing Germany.

b) The Mood in Britain

Most people in Britain now favoured standing firm against the dictators. There were demands for tougher words and actions, including faster rearmament, alliance with Russia, a broadening of the National Government and the inclusion in it of Winston Churchill, who was seen as a consistently strong opponent of Hitler. Chamberlain was aware of the pressure from his own party, and from the country at large. At the end of March 1939 his government announced the doubling of the territorial army. In April conscription was introduced for the first time in peacetime.

c) Hitler's Actions

Hitler used the announcement of the introduction of conscription in Britain to repudiate the Anglo-German Naval Agreement of 1935. He emphasised his desire for friendship with Britain, but he insisted that, just as he did not interfere in British policy in Palestine and elsewhere, so Britain had no right to interfere with German policy in her sphere of influence. In May 1939 Hitler told his generals he intended to attack Poland 'at the first available opportunity' but that he was still hopeful of detaching Britain and France from Poland and thus averting a general European war. Meanwhile German diplomats worked hard and with some success to secure support from (or improve relations with) a host of countries in Europe, including Sweden, Denmark, Latvia, Estonia, Hungary, Yugoslavia, Rumania, Bulgaria and Finland. They also worked to bring Japan into the Pact of Steel.

In June, Goebbels, the German Minister of Propaganda, conducted an anti-British campaign, denouncing Britain's encirclement policy and war-mongering. As the summer wore on there was increasing tension over Danzig. The Germans claimed that the British guarantee resulted in Poland refusing reasonable terms. They also accused Poland of launching a reign of terror against the German minority in Poland. These stories, although exaggerated, had a foundation of truth. There were anti-German demonstrations in many Polish cities and the Poles did arrest German nationalists and close down German schools and businesses. Thousands of Germans fled from Poland to Germany.

The Polish government continued to make it clear that it had no intention of giving in to Hitler. Most Poles believed that if they stood firm they could call Hitler's bluff. They had no wish to go the way of Austria and Czechoslovakia and were prepared to fight, if needs be, to maintain their country's independence.

d) Chamberlain's Position

Everything now depended on Hitler. There was little Chamberlain could do beyond stressing Britain's determination to stand by her new commitments. To make matters worse for the Prime Minister, in 1939 relations between Britain and Japan declined to a new low. Japan, critical of British economic and moral support for China, imposed a blockade on Tientsin, an important centre of British trade in China. There seemed a possibility of war. Given the situation in Europe, Britain had little alternative but to attempt to reach agreement with Japan, and in the late summer of 1939 relations between the two countries did improve. However, considerable problems remained, not least because Japan was still bent on a policy of expansion.

Chamberlain was less active in foreign policy in the summer of 1939 than at any time since 1937. However, he had not given up all hope of peace or of appeasement. He still thought there was a chance that Hitler would come to see that nothing would be gained by force which might not be gained by negotiation. As late as July 1939 energetic efforts were made to see if German colonial and economic ambitions could be met without sacrificing the vital interests of the western powers. Chamberlain was appalled at the prospect of war. Even so, Britain and France spent much of the summer preparing mobilisation and evacuation plans and coordinating their military preparations. It was evident to most people, including Chamberlain, that Britain might well be drawn into war over Poland.

5 Anglo-Soviet Relations

a) Relations 1931–8

A big question still remained: how could Britain and France actually help Poland if Germany attacked her? French plans were simply to mobilise behind their Maginot line defences. It would take Britain months – indeed years – to mobilise fully. Only the USSR could offer Poland immediate military help. Most French and many British politicians, especially those on the left, thought the only sensible course of action was to forge an alliance with the USSR.

For most of the 1920s and 1930s British governments, dominated by the Conservatives, had shown no wish to reach an agreement, or even establish much contact, with the USSR (see Chapter 2). The Soviet Union, both as a state and as the centre of an international revolutionary movement, was seen as hostile and dangerous to traditional British values and interests. Indeed many Conservatives considered communism a more serious threat than fascism, and regarded Nazi Germany as a useful bulwark against the threat of Soviet expansion.

However, in 1934–5 there was the prospect of some improvement in Anglo-Soviet relations. Faced with the threat of Hitler, the USSR abandoned its opposition to the League of Nations and became an enthusiastic supporter of the principle of collective security. In 1935 she signed defence pacts with France and Czechoslovakia and suggested high-level talks between Soviet and British diplomats. However, the USSR failed to weld a powerful alliance capable of deterring or defeating Nazi aggression. After 1935 neither the French nor the Russian governments made any real efforts to strengthen the defence pact. Russia had her own internal problems, while France had no wish to anger Britain, Italy and Poland, all of whom disapproved of the Franco-Soviet agreement.

The British government continued to oppose any alliance with the USSR. British policy was to isolate Russia and to keep her out of the international arena. Many Conservatives were angered by the fact that Russia gave support to the Republicans in the Spanish Civil War, and some preferred a compromise deal with Germany to cooperation with the USSR. Both Baldwin and Chamberlain suspected that the real aim of Soviet policy was to embroil Britain and France in a war against Germany and Italy, a war from which the USSR was likely to reap the most benefit.

Little effort had been made to secure Russian cooperation in 1938. Russia's appeal for an international conference immediately after the Anschluss was dismissed as premature by the British Foreign Office and was not even discussed by the Cabinet. Soviet approaches to Britain and France during the Czechoslovakian crisis were ignored. Stalin was not invited to attend the Munich Conference.

b) Chamberlain's Policy in 1939

In 1939 Chamberlain had no desire to ally with Russia. He distrusted Stalin and feared and hated the Soviet state and system. In March he expressed his thoughts about the USSR:

1 I must confess to the most profound distrust of Russia. I have no
  belief in her ability to maintain an effective offensive, even if she
  wanted to. And I distrust her motives, which seem to me to have
  little connection with our ideas of liberty and to be concerned
5 only with getting everyone else by the ears.

In Chamberlain's view, there were many good reasons for not allying with Russia. He believed that a policy of 'encirclement' of Germany – as in 1914 – could be counter-productive. It might lead to, rather than prevent, war. British military intelligence indicated that, after Stalin's purges, Russian forces were of little military value. 80 per cent of all Russia's senior army officers had been killed or imprisoned. It was also likely that a Russian agreement might alienate those east European countries that Britain was trying to win over. These states had no wish to reach agreement with Russia, particularly if that agreement involved Russian troops occupying their soil. They feared, with some justification, that once Russian troops were there, it would be difficult to remove them. There was the added risk that an Anglo-Russian alliance might drive Spain and Japan into the arms of Hitler.

Chamberlain was not alone in viewing Stalin with suspicion. F.A. Voight, foreign correspondent for the *Manchester Guardian*, summed up the situation in March 1939:

1 We ought, I think, to be critical about Russia. We need her and it
  isn't the time for polemics against her. But we must not, in my
  opinion, refer to her as a democracy – she is more tyrannically
  governed than even Germany is. The number of people done to
5 death in Germany runs into thousands – in Russia tens of
  thousands. Altogether, the terror in Russia is such that persons
  living even under the Nazi terror could hardly conceive of such a
  thing. But we cannot afford to be particular about our allies,
  though we must, I think, always remain particular about our
10 friends.

In 1939 Stalin certainly had a far worse record of terror and mass-murder than Hitler. However, Stalin's terror was concealed, ignored or even justified by many on the left who ideologically preferred communism to fascism. Even those who viewed fascism and communism with equal distaste were more worried by Hitler's Germany than Stalin's Russia. In 1939, therefore, Chamberlain found himself at odds with public opinion in Britain. Most people supported some kind of deal with the USSR. This is evident from a number of opinion polls carried out at the time:

If there was a war between Germany and Russia, which side would you rather see win? (December 1938)
Germany 15%
Russia 85%
No opinion 10%

If you *had* to choose between Fascism and Communism which side would you choose? (January 1939)
Fascism 26%
Communism 74%
No answer 16%

Would you like to see Great Britain and Soviet Russia being more friendly to each other? (March 1939)
Yes 84%
No 7%
No opinion 9%

Are you in favour of a military alliance between Great Britain, France and Russia? (June 1939)
Yes 84%
No 9%
No opinion 7%

In 1939 Chamberlain was under considerable pressure, from France, from the press, from parliament and even from within his Cabinet, to establish closer relations with Russia. Lloyd George, in a speech in the House of Commons in May 1939, reflected the views of many:

1 The Polish army is a brave one, but in no way comparable to Germany's. If we are going in without the help of Russia, we are walking into a trap. It is the only country whose armies can get there. If Russia is not being brought into the matter because the
5 Poles feel that they do not want them there, it is for us to declare the conditions, and unless the Poles are prepared to accept the only conditions with which we can successfully help them, the responsibility must be theirs ... Without Russia, these three guarantees of help to Poland, Rumania and Greece, are the most
10 reckless commitments that any country has ever entered into. It is madness ... Did the General Staff advise the government before

they entered into these commitments that there was the slightest
chance of achieving victory? If they did they ought to be removed
from the War Office and confined to a lunatic asylum. They are
15 entirely impossible without Russia. I see no sign that the government has worked out this problem. What force can they put into
the field? How can they get there?

c) Anglo-Soviet Negotiations in 1939

In late April 1939 Chamberlain finally agreed to the opening of
negotiations with Russia. He did so without much conviction. He still
saw Hitler and Stalin as much-of-a-muchness and disliked being forced
to choose between them. He favoured 'association', not a fully-fledged
Soviet alliance. His main aims seem to have been to placate opposition
at home and to use the possibility of an Anglo-Soviet alliance as a
further warning to Hitler.

Soviet policy in 1939 is a subject of great debate, and Stalin's own
thinking remains a matter of guesswork. On the surface his position
was serious. Hitler was a sworn enemy of Bolshevism and Japan was a
threat to Russia in the east. Therefore, Stalin faced and feared a two
front war. He also feared that Hitler's eastwards expansion was being
encouraged by Britain and France. This had never been Chamberlain's
policy – although, in the interests of his country, perhaps it should have
been. Indeed from March 1939 Chamberlain, far from deliberately
encouraging Hitler to move eastwards, as many on the left then and
later charged him with, was actually committed to stopping him. This
gave Stalin some room for manoeuvre. He could afford to press for
favourable terms from the British and French governments, and also to
throw out feelers to Germany about a possible deal. He made it clear in
a speech in March 1939 that dealing with a fascist regime was no more
repugnant than dealing with liberal-democratic states. He was in a
position to keep his options open and see who would make the best
offer. Tactically Britain and France were worse off. They had the
disadvantage of seeking Soviet support after and not before the
guarantees to Poland.

The Anglo-Soviet discussions, starting in late April and continuing
throughout the summer, were complex and slow. British negotiators
refused Russian proposals, submitted counter-proposals, which were
unacceptable to the Russians, and then generally ended up accepting
Russia's first proposals. Halifax was invited to Moscow but he declined
the invitation. Eden offered to go to Moscow on a special mission but
Chamberlain turned down his offer. Chamberlain himself did virtually
nothing. He placed little value on the outcome of the negotiations and
admitted in private that he would not mind much if they broke down.

His main purpose was to warn Hitler of the danger of Russia, rather than actually to ally with her.

A British and French military mission – which travelled by boat and train, rather than plane – finally arrived in Moscow in early August. The British mission was led by Admiral Reginald Aylmer Ranfurly Pluckett-Ernle-Erle-Drax, a man whose name was more impressive than his military importance. The French had instructions to secure the signing of a military convention in the minimum of time. On the other hand, British military representatives had been instructed to go 'very slowly'. The talks got nowhere. The western powers were not eager to trust the Soviet general staff with secret military plans and tried to keep the discussions on the plane of general principles rather than precise plans. The talks deadlocked when the Russians asked whether Poland would accept the entry of Russian troops before the event of a German attack. The Poles, deeply suspicious of Russian intentions, would not budge on this issue. 'We have no military agreement with the Russians', said Beck. 'We do not wish to have one.' Chamberlain sympathised with Poland, and did not see why the presence of Russian troops in Poland should be necessary or desirable.

d) The Nazi-Soviet Pact

The Soviet government maintained that it was the attitude of the western powers to the question of the entry of Russian troops into Poland which convinced them that Britain and France were not in earnest in their negotiations. However, it is equally possible that the military discussions were a shameless deception, that the Russians simply made a series of demands that they knew Britain and France could not accept, and that Stalin, courted by Germany, had no wish for an alliance with the West.

From 1933 the USSR had occasionally made approaches to Germany suggesting the need for improved relations. The Nazis had rebuffed each of these initiatives. The idea of a Nazi-Soviet agreement made no sense at all in ideological terms. However, in 1939 Hitler realised that a deal with Stalin would very much strengthen his position – at least in the short-term. Hitler was confident that a Nazi-Soviet agreemenet would frighten Britain and France into backing out of their undertakings to Poland. In January 1939, therefore, German diplomats began to make overtures to Russia.

The Russian response was favourable and German-Soviet talks began. By mid-August agreement on economic issues had been reached and the Germans proposed that Ribbentrop should visit Moscow to settle political matters. With his planned invasion of Poland less than a week away, Hitler sent a personal message to Stalin asking if Ribbentrop could visit Moscow by 23 August at the latest. Stalin reacted quickly and favourably. Ribbentrop flew to Moscow and on 23 August signed the Nazi-Soviet non-aggression pact. Secret clauses of the pact divided Poland and eastern Europe into spheres of German and Russian influence.

News of the Nazi-Soviet Pact came as a bombshell in London. Britain had received reports of the Russo-German talks, but most experts dismissed as unthinkable the idea that the great ideological enemies could reach agreement.

Much criticism has been levelled at Chamberlain for his failure to secure a Russian alliance. Certainly he had little enthusiasm for the Grand Alliance of Poland, Russia, France and Britain envisaged by Winston Churchill and others. However, such an alliance was probably beyond even the most determined and skilled British statesman. Poland was not interested in a Russian alliance and there is considerable evidence that the Russians had no wish for an alliance with the western powers. Stalin had no love of Britain or France. The only thing the West had to offer him was the prospect of immediate war, a war in which Russia would do most of the fighting. On the other hand, Hitler offered peace and territory. It is difficult to see how any British government could have matched the German offer – Soviet supremacy over the Baltic States and eastern Poland. From Stalin's point of view the Nazi-Soviet Pact seemed to best protect Soviet interests, at least in the short-term.

The Nazi-Soviet Pact was undoubtedly a decisive event. When Hitler heard news of the signing of the pact over dinner he banged the table in delight and shouted, 'I have them!' He realised that Poland could not now be defended and thought that Britain and France would realise the same. The way was open for the German attack on Poland, planned to start at 4.30am on 26 August.

6 The Outbreak of War

Hitler was prepared to gamble on – but still did not expect or want – a war on two fronts. He thought the British and French leaders were 'little worms' who would find a way to wriggle out of their commitments to Poland. However, Chamberlain had no intention of abandoning Poland. The Nazi-Soviet Pact did not unduly worry the British Prime Minister. He believed that Britain, France and Poland were strong enough to deter Hitler. Nor could he have made his intentions much clearer. On 22 August he sent a personal letter to Hitler stating explicitly that Britain would fight if Germany attacked Poland. On 25 August Britain and Poland signed a treaty of alliance. French politicians also made it clear that France would stand firm.

Hitler, surprised by the Anglo-French determination, was also shaken by Mussolini's announcement that Italy intended to remain neutral, despite the Pact of Steel. The German leader decided to postpone his invasion for five or six days, hoping in the meantime to detach the western powers from Poland. He made an extraordinary proposal to Britain. If Britain was prepared to give Germany a free-hand in Danzig and the Corridor, he would agree to guarantee the British Empire and try to reach agreement on disarmament. The British government saw this overture more as a divisive ploy than as a serious basis for negotiation. Britain confirmed that Poland would agree to negotiate with Germany but insisted that Britain would only accept a settlement which respected Poland's vital interests. By now Hitler had regained his nerve. He ordered the attack on Poland to begin on 1 September.

There were flurries of desperate last-minute diplomatic activity. Hitler hoped that Britain might have its price for Poland as it had for Czechoslovakia. Chamberlain, like most British and French politicians, hoped for peace. Lines of contact were kept open with Berlin in case Hitler should have a sudden change of heart. Poland was urged to avoid provocation and fresh incidents. On 29 August Hitler demanded that a Polish plenipotentiary be sent to Berlin on 30 August to receive the German terms relating to Danzig and the Polish Corridor. Perhaps this proposal was expected to be taken seriously; but perhaps it was intended to drive a wedge between Britain and Poland by demonstrating German reasonableness. Lord Halifax believed that the terms were not unreasonable but that the German timescale – 24 hours – certainly was. Britain and France put very little pressure on the Polish government, which decided not to comply with the German demands.

On 31 August Mussolini proposed that a conference should meet to try to resolve the Polish crisis. This sounded ominously like a second Munich. However, this time Mussolini's proposal came too late. That same evening Germany claimed that one of its wireless stations near the Polish border had been attacked by Poles. This claim, which was totally fabricated, was used as the excuse for war. At 4.45am on 1 September German troops invaded Poland and German planes bombed Warsaw.

Chamberlain was ready, if necessary, to honour Britain's commitment to Poland but hoped there might be a last minute reprieve. Mussolini persisted with his conference proposal and Bonnet, the French Foreign Minister, was reasonably enthusiastic. However, Britain insisted that a condition for such a conference was withdrawal of German troops from Poland. If Germany did not suspend hostilities, Britain 'warned' Germany that she would fight. But on 2 September – a day and a half after the German attack – Britain still had not declared war or even sent an ultimatum to Germany. The reason for this delay was almost certainly Chamberlain's wish to keep in step with France. The French were anxious to complete their general mobilisation process before declaring war. However, it seemed to many British politicians as though the Prime Minister was trying to evade his commitments.

On 2 September Chamberlain told the House of Commons that he was still prepared to forget everything that had happened if Germany agreed to withdraw her forces from Poland. He made no mention of an ultimatum to Germany. This did not satisfy many of the Prime Minister's critics. Both Labour and Conservative MPs made clear their opinion that war must be declared at once. At a Cabinet meeting later that evening Chamberlain accepted the inevitable. At 9.00am on 3 September Britain finally delivered an ultimatum to Germany. Germany made no reply and at 11.00am Britain declared war. France followed suit and declared war at 5.00pm. Britain's declaration of war automatically brought in India and the colonies. The Dominions were free to decide for themselves, but within one week Australia, New Zealand, South Africa and Canada had all declared war on Germany.

Chamberlain had been forced into a war which he and the British public had always wanted to avoid. However, in September 1939 most people in Britain seem to have accepted the necessity for war. Replies to a Gallup Poll question at the end of September showed 89 per cent of the British people in favour of 'fighting until Hitlerism was done away with'. The wording of the Poll question might have been ambiguous, but there seems little doubt about the resolve of the British public.

7 An Assessment of Neville Chamberlain

a) The Case against Neville Chamberlain

For many years after 1939 Neville Chamberlain was criticised as one of the main 'guilty men' who had failed to stand up to Adolf Hitler. The views of Sir Winston Churchill carried great weight and shaped much historical thinking. Churchill thought the Second World War 'unnecessary' and subtitled his book, *The Gathering Storm*, 'How the English-speaking peoples through their unwisdom, carelessness and good nature allowed the wicked to rearm'. In consequence, Chamberlain has often been depicted as one of the great 'losers' of modern British history – a rather pathetic old man whose policies helped to cause the Second World War. The criticisms of Chamberlain are many, varied and conflicting! (See the summary chart.)

The main criticism of Chamberlain is that he tried to appease Hitler. Many historians think this made little sense. Hitler made no secret of his aim to dominate Europe and the world. He was a ruthless tyrant who was prepared to use war to achieve his evil ends. In consequence the only correct policy was to stand firm against him at the earliest opportunity. Appeasement simply whetted his appetite and encouraged him to make fresh demands. With each surrender Germany grew stronger and more dangerous. Some historians blame Chamberlain not so much for his policy of appeasement, but for his failure to stand by it to the end. They see his policy falling between two stools, with the result that Britain stumbled into a disastrous war against Germany, a war which Britain should have avoided at all costs. He is particularly criticised for allying with Poland. Some historians think that Britain had no moral obligation or self-evident interest to fight a major war over Poland. In 1939 the Germans had a good case. Poland was ruled by a right-wing dictatorship. Annexation of Poland would not necessarily have strengthened Germany. It would simply have brought her face to face with Russia.

It has been argued that Chamberlain should have allowed – even encouraged – Hitler to expand eastwards, and thus ultimately to fight Russia. It is true that Britain and France might have been in danger if Germany had defeated Russia; Hitler could have followed a Russian victory by an attack to the west. But all this is far from certain. Would Hitler have beaten Russia? And if he had done so, would this have strengthened or weakened Germany? It is possible to claim that Britain had little to lose and much to gain from a German-Russian war.

In the end the main indictment against Chamberlain is that he failed. In September 1939 Britain was forced into war – a war in which she had little to gain and everything to lose. Chamberlain himself admitted that everything he had hoped for and believed in had 'crashed in ruins'.

b) The Case for Neville Chamberlain

Over the last two decades historians have tended to view Chamberlain in a far more sympathetic light. Most historians accept that Chamberlain had very little room for manoeuvre. Many think he pursued clear, rational policies. Most of the charges against him can be answered and much can be said in his defence. (See the summary chart.)

Appeasement was a logical policy to follow both before and after 1937. The policy of avoiding confrontation by negotiation and concession was a deep-rooted British tradition (and remains a fundamental purpose of diplomacy today). Chamberlain saw appeasement not as surrender but as a positive effort to achieve a settlement of all the difficult issues which had plagued Europe since 1919. Like many people in Britain, he felt that Germany had some legitimate grievances. Justice did not become injustice because it was demanded by a dictator. Moreover, Chamberlain realised that there was no practical alternative to appeasement. After 1935 Germany could not have been challenged without the real risk of a long and bloody war, a war for which Britain was woefully unprepared and which she might not win. Britain had little to gain from even a successful war. 750,000 British lives had been lost in the First World War. Another conflict might well result in an even greater loss of life. It would also be ruinessly expensive and seriously damage Britain's economic position.

Chamberlain seems to have had few illusions about Hitler. He feared his ambition and unpredictability. However, he realised that he was not in a position to get rid of the German leader and thus had little alternative but to work with him. He hoped that active diplomacy could reduce the threat of war.

In the event Chamberlain's policies failed and Britain did go to war with Germany. However, the situation might have been worse. Britain and France were firmly allied and stronger than ever before. They had more tanks and troops than Germany and would soon have more planes. Their economic strength was much greater. They also had what seemed like a useful ally in Poland, who they hoped might keep Germany occupied until at least the spring of 1940. In 1939, Hitler was effectively isolated. Both Italy and Japan had misgivings about the direction of German policy and were not prepared (as yet) to risk war with Britain. The British people and the Dominions were united in favour of the war in a way that seemed inconceivable in 1938. Most people felt the time had come to resist German expansion. Every effort had been made to satisfy German grievances, but Hitler had proved that he could not be trusted. Enough was enough, and to do nothing was simply to put off the evil hour. The French government and most French people reached the same conclusion.

Chamberlain may not have been totally exonerated by recent historians, but most see him as a helpless rather than a 'guilty' man. He thought of himself as a typical Englishman, upright and honourable, a man of brains and common sense. Perhaps his estimate of himself was not so far wrong! Appeasement seems more sensible now than it did a generation ago, and it was certainly not a policy of shameful cowardice. Like most British, French and American politicians and people, Chamberlain believed that appeasement was the best policy in the circumstances of the time. Its chances of working were good enough to warrant giving it every opportunity. The fact that it failed does not mean that it was not worth attempting.

Most historians would agree that the ambitions of Hitler, and not the mistakes of Chamberlain, are largely responsible for the outbreak of war in 1939. Debate about the nature of the Nazi regime and Hitler's precise aims rages on. However, there seems little doubt that Hitler was committed to expansion eastwards. His ideas of racial superiority and his relentless quest for 'living space' made war likely – especially as he was prepared to gamble and take risks for ever higher stakes. As a result, Europe stumbled from crisis to crisis. This built up an almost irresistible pressure for war by 1939.

For Hitler, war was a historical and racial necessity: the final test. If Britain and France were not prepared to accept German domination of eastern Europe, then he was ready to fight them. There was nothing accidental about Hitler's attack on Poland. He hoped the western powers would not join in, but he was prepared to take that risk. Given Hitler's aims it seems likely that war with Germany would have come sooner or later whoever had been in power in Britain. Whether Britain would have been better fighting sooner than 1939 – or later – is a debate which will continue.

To the end Chamberlain could see no alternatives to the policies which he had pursued. In September 1939, in a radio speech to the British people on the outbreak of war, he said, 'You can imagine what a bitter blow it is to me that all my long struggle to win peace has failed. Yet I cannot believe that there is anything more or anything different that I could have done that would have been more successful.' Many historians agree with this verdict.

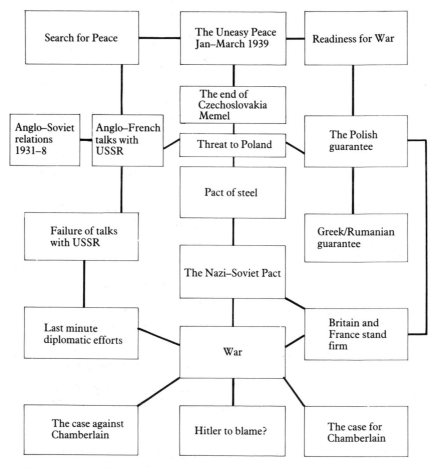

Summary – The Coming of War, 1939

NEVILLE CHAMBERLAIN

THE CASE AGAINST	THE CASE FOR
Tried to appease an unappeasable Hitler – appeasement simply encouraged Hitler to make new demands – correct policy: firmness	Appeasement was logical – Germany had legitimate grievances – the only alternative was war (for which Britain was unprepared) – negotiation and concession better than confrontation.
Weak and indecisive (Hitler and Mussolini's view)	Strong, ruthless, successful politician
Little diplomatic experience Easily duped	Well-informed on foreign matters. Did not trust Hitler or Mussolini

Autocratic, pig-headed
Surrounded by 'yes' men
Refused to listen to critics
eg Churchill
    Labour Party
	Prepared to change his policies (eg 1939)
	Listened to views different to his own (eg Lord Halifax's)
	His critics not worth listening to: Churchill – a war monger!
	    Labour Party – favoured war and disarmament

Conducted foreign policy on his own ignoring advice of:
    Foreign Office
    Cabinet
    Parliament
    The British people
	Chamberlain's foreign policy was in line with the views of:
	    Foreign Office
	    Cabinet
	    Parliament
	    The British people

Munich: a disaster – sacrificed an ally – Britain and allies better prepared for war in 1938 than 1939	Munich: a triumph – Hitler backed down – averted war – Britain and allies better prepared in 1939 than 1938
Failed to ensure Britain re-armed	Did more than any politician to ensure Britain was ready for war
Failed to build a 'Grand Alliance' with the USSR and the USA	A 'Grand Alliance' was impossible. The USSR could not be trusted The USA had no interest in an alliance

His policy fell between 'two stools' – he should not have abandoned appeasement and allied with Poland in 1939 – Germany had a good case in 1939 – Hitler was no immediate threat to Britain – Britain should have encouraged Hitler to go eastwards – against Russia	He had to stand firm in 1939: – the aim of the Polish alliance was to deter Hitler, not bring about war – Hitler wanted all of Poland, not just Danzig – If Germany defeated Poland (and Russia) she would dominate Europe and threaten Britain

Making notes on 'The Coming of War'

Your notes on this chapter (and the last) should give you an understanding of the events that led Britain to declare war on Nazi Germany in September 1939 and enable you to assess the wisdom of appeasement and the statesmanship of Neville Chamberlain. As you read the chapter try to identify what Chamberlain could have done that was different. Could and should war have been averted? Should Chamberlain have gone to war sooner? To what extent was Chamberlain to blame for the Second World War?

It is also worth studying the map on page 116 so that you are familiar with the countries and areas mentioned in the text.

Answering essay questions on 'The Coming of War, 1939'

It is unlikely that you will be asked for a narrative of the events from Munich to the outbreak of war. More likely you will need to use evidence from this chapter (and the previous two) to answer specific questions about the wisdom or foolishness of appeasement. Three typical examples of such questions are:

1 Was there ever any real alternative to Chamberlain's policy of appeasing the European dictators?
2 Were there sound strategic reasons for the appeasement of Germany in the 1930s?

3 'A mistaken policy followed by honourable men for honourable ends'. Discuss this view of the policy of appeasement as followed during the 1930s.

All these questions are of the same basic type. They require you to construct a two part answer. One part argues 'Yes . . . appeasement was inevitable/sensible/honourable etc . . . in these ways/to this extent.' The other part argues 'No . . . appeasement was not inevitable/sensible/honourable . . . in these ways/to this extent.'

Look at the first question. Make a list of reasons to support the argument that there were sound alternatives to Chamberlain's policy of appeasement. Then make a second list, this time in defence of Chamberlain's policy and the problems with the alternative policies. Decide whether you will argue in support of Chamberlain (ie there were few better alternative policies) or against him (ie there were some alternative policies that were better than appeasement).

It might be helpful to write the essay. Remember it is often good tactics to present the arguments you don't really agree with first; you can then use the second part of the essay to say why not, and to put forward the arguments you tend to favour. Try to present a balanced, reasoned argument but don't be afraid to 'come off the fence' – providing you can support your arguments with sound evidence and display an awareness of the arguments of the other point of view.

You might also have to answer other types of questions on appeasement. Look at the following questions:

4 'Buying time for rearmament.' Is this description of Britain's policy of appeasing the fascist dictators from 1937 justified?
5 Why and in what ways did Britain pursue a policy of appeasement in the 1930s?
6 To what extent and for what reasons was there support in Britain for the Government's policy of appeasing Hitler?

All these questions are concerned with the reasons why Chamberlain – and many others – supported appeasement. Look at question 4. Make a list of the main points you would wish to make if you were answering this question. Do you agree with the statement about 'buying time'? In what ways would your answer to this question be i) similar and ii) different to your answer to question 1?

Source-based questions on 'The Coming of War, 1939'

1 Chamberlain's Birmingham Speech, March 1939
Read the extract from Chamberlain's speech to the Unionist Association at Birmingham on pages 117–8 and examine the cartoon on page 121. Answer the following questions:
a) Why did Chamberlain see Hitler's occupation of Prague as different to the previous 'unpleasant surprises' Hitler had sprung upon the world? (3 marks)
b) What main point was Chamberlain making to his audience, and perhaps to Hitler, in this speech? (2 marks)
c) What motives did Chamberlain have for making this particular speech at this particular time? (4 marks)
d) What point is the cartoon trying to make? Does the cartoon suggest that Chamberlain had got his point across to Hitler in April 1939? (6 marks)

2 British Views on Russia in 1939
Read Chamberlain's, Voight's and Lloyd George's views of Russia (pages 125–7) and examine the results of the opinion polls (page 126). Answer the following questions:
a) To what extent did Chamberlain and Voight agree? (2 marks)
b) What is their major point of difference? (3 marks)
c) What was the main point Lloyd George was making? In what way does the Chamberlain extract cast doubt on Lloyd George's viewpoint? (4 marks)
d) Why do you think so many British people in 1939 seem to have preferred Stalin to Hitler? (5 marks)
e) To what extent might the results of opinion polls such as these have influenced Chamberlain's policy to Russia in 1939? Do you think opinion polls should have affected his policy? Explain your answers. (6 marks)

CHAPTER 7

Conclusion

1 The Guilty Men?

Most historians have been critical of the conduct of British foreign
policy in the inter-war period. This is not too surprising. In 1919
Britain emerged as the victor in the First World War. Yet only 20 years
later, she found herself engaged in a Second World War. By the time
this war ended in 1945 Britain was no longer the great superpower she
had appeared to be in 1919. It seems obvious that British governments
and statesmen in the inter-war period must be held responsible. In
March 1938 Winston Churchill said in the House of Commons:

> 1 . . . if mortal catastrophe should overtake the British Nation and
> the British Empire, historians a thousand years hence will still be
> baffled by the mystery of our affairs. They will never understand
> how it was that a victorious nation, with everything in hand,
> 5 suffered themselves to be brought low, and to cast away all that
> they had gained by measureless sacrifice and absolute victory –
> gone with the wind!
> Now the victors are the vanquished, and those who threw down
> their arms in the field and sued for an armistice are striding on to
> 10 world mastery . . .

Many historians have criticised successive governments for failing to
face up to the evil personified by Hitler, for drift, for not rearming
sufficiently, for failing to ally with the USA or the USSR, and for
allowing Germany to become a threat to world peace. The prime
ministers of the 1930s – Ramsay MacDonald, Stanley Baldwin and
Neville Chamberlain – have been particularly blamed.

However, it is possible to question the extent to which inter-war
statesmen in general, and MacDonald, Baldwin and Chamberlain in
particular, should be blamed for adopting misguided policies. This final
chapter will consider several issues which are of crucial importance in
considering British statesmen's collective or individual culpability.
These are:

a) To what extent did 'strong' prime ministers actually control or
'make' foreign policy?
b) To what extent did Britain have the power to be able to influence
world events?
c) What alternatives were open to Britain, especially in the 1930s?

2 Who made British Foreign Policy?

The central column of policy-making machinery extended down from the Prime Minister, through the Cabinet and Foreign Office to British diplomatic missions around the world. The relationship between prime minister and foreign secretary was crucial. Baldwin abandoned a great deal of responsibility to his foreign secretaries (especially Austen Chamberlain) and was quite prepared, for example, to let Sir Samuel Hoare take the blame in 1935. At the other extreme, Neville Chamberlain and Ramsay MacDonald, like Lloyd George before them, tried to run their own foreign policies and, as a result, sometimes came into conflict with their foreign secretaries (Chamberlain, for example, found himself at odds with Eden in 1937–8). Usually, however, prime ministers chose foreign secretaries whom they could trust and to whom they felt able to delegate substantial authority.

Prime ministers (and their foreign secretaries) undoubtedly made important decisions. However, the shaping of British foreign policy did not totally depend on their actions. All prime ministers and foreign secretaries had to consider the views of other members of the Cabinet. It is true that most of the time the Cabinet as a whole had relatively little say on foreign policy matters, if only because few diplomatic issues actually reached Cabinet level. However, all prime ministers realised the necessity of having the support of most of the Cabinet, particularly on key foreign issues. Even Neville Chamberlain, a 'strong' prime minister, frequently heeded the advice of his Cabinet, and sometimes against his better judgement. Members of all governments saw themselves as a team, and unity was a foremost consideration. When real disagreement was evident, there were invariably attempts to build a consensus and to reconcile divisions.

The Cabinet was ultimately responsible to Parliament. Although Parliament rarely intervened in day-to-day foreign affairs, many individual MPs (like Churchill) were very interested in foreign policy developments and often questioned the wisdom of government policy. In the last resort Parliament could force governments to take particular courses of action. For example, given the feeling in the House of Commons, Chamberlain would have found it very difficult not to have declared war on Germany on 3 September 1939.

Parliament, in turn, represented public opinion. The public as a whole was rarely interested in the details of foreign policy. However, public opinion did set the broad ideological framework within which foreign policy had to operate. Most people in Britain in the inter-war years, for example, preferred governments to spend money on health, social services and education rather than on defence. The public could not be ignored by political parties whose main purpose was to win elections. In the early 1930s successive British governments had to be seen to be supporting the League of Nations and the idea of collective security, both popular with the electorate. In 1939 Chamberlain may have been persuaded to take a tougher line against Hitler by the pressure of public opinion. He could certainly not have risked going to war in 1939 unless he was certain he had the firm support of the majority of the country.

The public, in turn, were influenced by the mass media, particularly by the press but increasingly in the 1930s by radio and newsreels which people saw when they went (as they did frequently in the 1920s and 1930s) to the cinema. To what extent the media were influenced by – or influenced – both the government and public opinion is keenly debated by historians. The media were certainly in a position to shape the agenda of public debate by focusing on certain news items and giving them particular colouring and significance. In the 1930s, for example, newsreels invariably showed ranks of marching soldiers when reporting on Nazi Germany. This gave the impression that Nazi Germany was more a militarised state than was perhaps the case.

Some historians think foreign policy-making was as much in the hands of professional career civil servants in the Foreign Office as politicians. Robert Vansittart, Permanent Under-Secretary of State in the Foreign Office 1930–8, was certainly able to exert considerable control over foreign policy. Other Whitehall departments – the India Office, the Colonial Office, the Dominion Office (set up in 1925), the War Office, the Admiralty and the Air Ministry – also influenced foreign policy-making. Treasury officials, because they were in a position to scrutinise any proposal involving government spending, also had considerable authority. Therefore foreign policy-making was handled by a plethora of rival civil service departments, each with its own specialists, who remained at their post whoever was in office. Some historians think that the existence of this entrenched bureaucracy resulted in continuity, compromise and lower common-denominator policies which satisfied most interests to some degree but which may have prevented radical changes of policy.

Many of the senior civil servants came from similar backgrounds to the politicians. They attended the same public schools (especially Eton and Harrow) and the same Universities (overwhelmingly Oxford and Cambridge), and often frequented the same London clubs. Some historians think that this 'elite' controlled foreign policy in their own 'class' interests. This conclusion is perhaps too sweeping, as it does not account for the fact that many of the so-called elite had very different views on many foreign policy issues.

The final – and obvious – point is that British foreign policy was largely shaped and determined by the actions of non-Britons. British prime ministers, foreign secretaries, Cabinets, Parliaments, public opinion, media or civil servants had no real control over the policies of Hitler, Stalin, Mussolini or the Japanese militarists. In fact, Britain could not even exert much influence over the policies of more friendly governments, such as those of France and the USA. British foreign policy-makers had to respond to the real (and potential) actions of a variety of powers, both friendly and hostile.

3 Was Britain Great?

In 1939 few doubted that Britain was still a great power. She controlled a massive Empire, had the world's strongest navy, and was the world's greatest trading nation. Her economy was strong enough to bind all the countries of the Empire to the British imperial system. Both colonies and Dominions relied on British markets for their principal exports, for banking facilities, for investment, and on British manufactured goods. Although Hitler was prepared to risk war against Britain, he hoped until the very end to avert such a conflict.

However, Britain was not as 'great' as some politicians at the time imagined. Britain's power needs to be seen in relation to that of other countries. By the 1930s Russia, Germany and France all had far larger and stronger armies that Britain. The USA and Japan had powerful navies. The USA was economically stronger than Britain. Germany produced more coal, iron and steel. Although Russia took some time to recover from the Bolshevik Revolution and the Civil War which followed, Stalin's Five Year Plans led to a great increase in Russian industrial production. The USA, Russia and Germany all had much larger populations.

The British Empire gave Britain the appearance of being a really great world power. In 1932, at its peak, the Empire covered nearly one quarter of the earth's land surface and included a quarter of the world's population. However, the Empire was not as strong as many Britons hoped or imagined. By 1931 the most developed parts of the Empire – the 'white' Dominions – were effectively independent. This meant that, unlike 1914, in the event of war Britain could no longer take their support for granted. Many Afrikaaner South Africans and French Canadians had no love for Britain. The same was even more true of the southern Irish. British control of India was similarly superficial. It very much depended on the Indians themselves, and they were growing increasingly restive. By 1939 the granting of dominion status to India seemed highly likely, if not inevitable. Much of the rest of the Empire was underdeveloped. British colonial policy in the inter-war years was essentially one of benevolent neglect. Given that Britain put so little in, she could expect to get little out. Therefore the 'great' British Empire was something of a 'paper tiger'. Indeed some historians view the over-extended Empire as a strategic liability, rather than a strength.

Britain's relative economic decline, evident to many observers from the late nineteenth century, was a major problem. Wealth usually determines power and Britain's declining ability to shape world affairs owed much to a diminution in its relative economic strength. During the inter-war years historians have seen the country suffering from a variety of economic ills. Some have stressed poor management, an inability to exploit new ideas, outdated technology, poor salesmanship and a low rate of investment. Others have stressed overpowerful trade unions, shoddy workmanship and bad labour relations.

It is possible to overstate Britain's economic decline. Protectionist policies and preferential trade with the Dominions helped to sustain British industry through the harsh economic climate of the 1930s. However, other countries were overtaking British industrial production and squeezing Britain's share of world trade. In the 1930s Britain started to have a persistent balance of payments deficit, reflecting both its weakening competitive position industrially and the reduction of its invisible earnings. Throughout the period the country found it difficult to get rid of the intractable problem of unemployment which reached its peak at 3,000,000 in the early 1930s. Britain's economic difficulties reduced her capacity to maintain or increase her armaments.

There was another defence problem. For hundreds of years Britain had been able to rely on naval power for security. Battleships however, were no longer sufficient. During the First World War German submarines had threatened to starve Britain into surrender. More serious still were aircraft developments. Enemy bombers could now leap-frog the English Channel. 'The old frontiers are gone', said Baldwin in 1934. 'When you think of the defence of England you no longer think of the chalk cliffs of Dover; you think of the Rhine'. Britain was no longer safe from attack. The pre-eminent position of London, home for one fifth of the British population, the centre of government, finance and trade, made it a more significant target than anywhere else in Europe. In 1937 the Chiefs of Staff estimated that there might be 20,000 casualties in London in the first 24 hours of war, rising to 150,000 within one week. In the end these estimates were way off target: civilian casualties in Britain during the whole of the Second World War from aerial bombing amounted to about 147,000. But Chamberlain was not to know that his military experts had exaggerated the effects of German bombing. In September 1938 Chamberlain told his Cabinet colleagues how he had looked down on London as he flew home from his second visit to Hitler and 'asked himself what degree of protection they could afford to the thousands of homes' spread out below. He concluded 'that we were in no position to justify waging a war today in order to prevent a war hereafter'.

In the 1920s Britain had enjoyed some freedom of manoeuvre to promote her world interests and shore-up her Empire without serious threat to her position. Germany was still recovering from her defeat in the First World War. Both the USA and the USSR, for very different reasons, withdrew from international diplomacy. However, in the 1930s Britain was threatened by the growing strength and ambitions of

Germany, Italy and Japan. She lacked the economic and military resources to meet – unassisted – the challenge of these potential rivals.

4 The World's Policeman?

Government critics in the 1930s, both on the left and right, continued to demand that Britain should play a tough world policeman role, taking on aggressors wherever they appeared. The left thought Britain should do this via the League of Nations, believing that the League would preserve peace without a special effort on anyone's part. Many on the left called for action against Germany, Italy and Japan and yet supported British disarmament. They imagined that moral force and the threat of sanctions would be sufficient to stop Hitler, Mussolini and/or the Japanese militarists.

The right appreciated the importance of force. However, politicians such as Churchill tended to overestimate Britain's strength. Churchill believed that Britain could and should have stopped Hitler and the other aggressors sooner. It is often forgotten that, in all probability, this would not have avoided war. Churchill's war – or wars – would simply have been fought sooner rather than later and it is far from certain that this would have been to Britain's advantage. At least by fighting when she did, ultimately Britain was on the winning side. In 1940–1 Churchill clung to the belief that 'given the tools' Britain could defeat a Germany which by then controlled most of Europe. In fact it was only alliance with the USSR and the USA that ensured that Britain was on the winning side in the Second World War.

British governments throughout the inter-war years were more realistic than their critics. They realised that they could not control events in Germany, Japan or Italy. They were aware of the fragility of British power and the degree to which it rested on appearances rather than on substance. They were aware of the disparity between Britain's world-wide commitments and her capacity to meet them. In the 1930s the Chiefs of Staff stressed repeatedly that Britain was incapable of defying Germany, Italy and Japan simultaneously. Aware of Britain's vulnerability and the fact that she had a vested interest in peace, British statesmen did their best to avoid conflict.

Perhaps British governments should have spent more on armaments, especially in the 1930s (there was little point in the 1920s). However, as Treasury officials argued, this would have weakened an already strained economy. In their view, economic strength was Britain's fourth arm of defence. Only if Britain was economically strong had she much hope of winning a war against Germany. Public opinion, which preferred government spending on social welfare to defence, was also a limiting factor. British attitudes (before 1939) made it impossible to consider the introduction of conscription. Therefore, Britain had no pool of semi-trained reserves that could be quickly made effective in the event of war.

5 Blame or Sympathy?

Throughout the inter-war period most governments had attempted to avoid Continental entanglements which might force Britain into war. In particular most British statesmen accepted that Britain had no great interests in central or eastern Europe. Danzig and the Polish Corridor, in Austen Chamberlain's view, were something 'for which no British government ever will or ever can risk the bones of a British grenadier'. Neville Chamberlain, Austen's half-brother, held very similar views. Somewhat ironically it was events in central and eastern Europe in 1938–9 that convinced Neville Chamberlain, and most Britons, that Hitler must be stopped. In September 1939 Britain went to war as a result of a quarrel between Germany and Poland over Danzig and the Polish Corridor. Since 1945 most historians have argued that Britain was right to go to war. The main debate has been whether Britain should have gone to war sooner than 1939.

However, Chamberlain's decisions to guarantee Poland's security in March 1939 and then to declare war on Germany in September 1939 can certainly be criticised. By allying with Poland, Britain broke one of the cardinal tenets of her foreign policy: no commitments in eastern Europe. British military chiefs were not consulted about the wisdom of guaranteeing the security of Poland (Greece and Rumania) and no staff talks followed the guarantees. By guaranteeing Poland, the British government had been shocked into doing what Chamberlain had firmly refused to do over Czechoslovakia, namely to leave Britain's decision for peace and war effectively in Hitler's hands. In 1939 Britain went to war, in A.J.P. Taylor's view, for 'that part of the peace settlement which they [British statesmen] had long regarded as least defensible'. Poland – corrupt, elitist and racist – was not a state that any nation could be proud of having to fight to save. Taylor's views, which are now supported by other historians, are worth serious consideration. What exactly had Britain to gain by going to war in 1939? How could she help Poland? Did British assurances of support encourage Poland to take an unreasonable and intransigent attitude to Germany? Was Hitler really an immediate threat to Britain? Might it not have been to Britain's advantage to encourage Hitler to keep pressing eastwards so that he would come-up against the USSR?

According to Winston Churchill when writing about his ancestor, the Duke of Marlborough, Britain invariably threw away the fruits of victory after a successful war. It is possible to levy this charge at British statesmen (collectively and individually) after the First World War – and Churchill, in particular, did so! Nevertheless it is important to realise the difficult problems British governments and statesmen faced.

Most statesmen – Churchill was an exception – realised that another world war, even a successful one, was the most likely way of throwing away the fruits of victory of the First World War. The much-maligned inter-war policy-makers did their best to avoid war. In the end circumstances – and Hitler – conspired against them and their best was not good enough. However, it is worth remembering that historians today, even with the benefit of hindsight, disagree about the best and wisest course of action. In the 1920s and 1930s statesmen had to respond to crises quickly and with little time for calm reflection. Nor did they have access to the range and quality of information available to later historians. In the circumstances British inter-war statesmen inevitably made mistakes. But, given the problems they faced, they would seem to deserve sympathy as well as, and perhaps even instead of, blame.

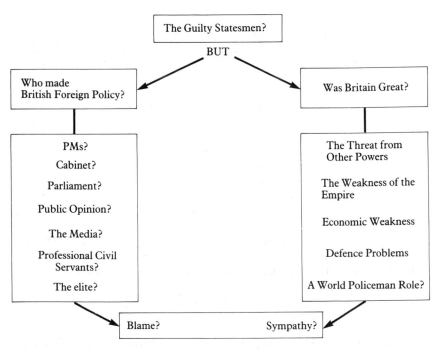

Summary – Conclusion

Making notes on 'Conclusion'

This chapter reconsiders many of the issues raised in chapter 1, and, in particular, assesses the extent to which British foreign policy-makers should be held responsible for the events which culminated in the outbreak of war in 1939. What mistakes did British statesmen make? Which individual was most to blame? Should anyone be blamed? These are questions which historians (and politicians!) still debate. Your notes should set out the extent to which British prime ministers (and/or foreign secretaries) controlled foreign policy and the problems which they faced. They should help you to reach your own conclusions about the skill – or otherwise – of British statesmen in the inter-war period.

Answering essay questions on 'Britain: Foreign and Imperial Policy 1919–39'

There are usually five main categories of essay question – 'What?', 'Why', 'How far/to what extent?', 'Assess' and 'The challenging statement'. Study the following questions and divide them into the five categories:

1 'Appeasement began long before Neville Chamberlain became Prime Minister.' How far is this a valid comment on Anglo-German relations between 1919 and 1937?
2 Why did Britain come to be involved in war in 1939?
3 Examine and explain the shifts and changes in British attitudes towards Germany from the Treaty of Versailles to the declaration of war in September 1939?
4 Can British policy towards Germany between 1919 and 1939 be defended?
5 'The Munich Agreement was unavoidable; the real mistakes were made before and afterwards.' Discuss this view.
6 What factors influenced Britain's policy towards Germany between the two World Wars?
7 Assess the policies of successive British governments to Germany from 1919 to 1939.

All these questions cover similar ground. However, they all have a slightly different emphasis and would need to be tackled in different ways. Which of the questions do you think is a) the easiest and b) the hardest – and why? Make a detailed plan for the question you consider the easiest.

Most students find the first and last paragraphs of essays the hardest to write. So let us finish with a difficult task! Plan introductions and conclusions for two questions for which you have not made a detailed plan. Note the extent of overlap, but also the way you need to stress different points.

Further Reading

You will not be surprised to learn that there are hundreds of excellent books on British foreign and imperial policy 1919–39. It is impossible for most students to consult more than a few of these. However, it is vital that you read some, particularly if you are taking the period as a special or depth study. It is a common complaint of all history examiners that candidates do not read widely enough. The following suggestions are meant to serve as a guide.

1 Textbooks
There are many general works on British history in this period. Among the best are:

C.L. Mowat, *Britain between the Wars* (Methuen 1955)
K.G. Robbins, *The Eclipse of a Great Power: Modern Britain 1870–1975* (Longman 1983)
A.J.P. Taylor, *English History 1914–1945* (Oxford University 1975)

Mowat and Robbins are 'safe', whereas A.J.P. Taylor is more controversial, irreverent and challenging.

2 Texts on British Foreign Policy
There are many general texts on British foreign policy between the wars. There is one book that is particularly worth reading. This is:

W. Churchill, *The Second World War: Vol 1 The Gathering Storm* (Cassell 1948)

For many years Churchill's views of events shaped historians' (and politicians') perceptions of British foreign policy-making in the inter-war period. You need to know what Churchill's views are, without necessarily agreeing with them!

The most accessible of the modern texts, giving more up-to-date interpretations on many of the relevant issues, include:

D. Reynolds, *Britannia Overruled: British Policy and World Power in the Twentieth Century* (Longman 1991)
P. Kennedy, *The Realities Behind Diplomacy* (Fontana 1981)
R. Douglas, *World Crisis and British Decline, 1929–56* (Macmillan 1986)

All three of these books examine British foreign policy in the twentieth century and try to account for Britain's (relative) 'decline'.

3 Texts on European Events
British foreign policy was not made in a vacuum. It is therefore well

worth your while to read some general books on foreign policy which do not focus specifically on Britain. One book which is particularly worth reading is:

A.J.P. Taylor, *The Origins of the Second World War* (Penguin 1961)

This book caused a storm of protest in the 1960s because Taylor argued that Hitler was far from solely to blame for the start of the Second World War. Read what Taylor has to say, but keep your critical wits about you and don't accept everything he says as gospel truth. However Taylor makes a number of very telling points which have stood the test of time.

A 'safer' text is:

P.M.H. Bell, *The Origins of the Second World War in Europe* (Longman 1986)

This provides a very thorough examination of the developments which led to the outbreak of the Second World War.

4 British Imperial Policy

Many books discuss Britain's relations with the dominions and colonies. Among the best are:

T.O. Lloyd, *The British Empire 1558–1983* (Oxford University 1984)

It is worth reading chapters 10 and 11 in particular.

J.G. Darwin, *Britain and Decolonisation* (Macmillan 1988)

A perceptive and persuasive book. Again you need read only a small part of it – in this case the first three or four chapters.

5 Appeasement

Texts on British appeasement include:

K. Robbins, *Appeasement* (Historical Association 1988)

This is a short and interesting read, especially for those who have already established the 'shape' of the topic in their minds.

W.R. Rock, *British Appeasement in the 1930s* (Edward Arnold 1977)

This book is generally critical of the appeasers.

6 More Specialist Works

Students who wish to track down more specialist works can most effectively start via the bibliographies in Taylor's (1975) and Reynolds' (1991) volumes.

Chronological Table

1914   August, start of the First World War.

1916   December, Lloyd George became PM.

1917   April, United States entered the war.
November, Bolshevik Revolution in Russia.

1918   November, end of First World War.
December, General Election. Victory for the Conservative-Liberal coalition. Lloyd George continued as PM.

1919   January, Paris Peace Conference began.
April, Amritsar Massacre.
June, Treaty of Versailles.
September, Treaty of St Germain (with Austria).
November, Treaty of Neuilly (with Bulgaria).

1920   June, Treaty of Trianon (with Hungary).
August, Treaty of Sevres (with Turkey).

1921   December, Anglo-Irish Treaty signed: creation of the Irish Free State.

1922   February, Washington Naval Agreement: America, Britain, Japan, France and Italy agreed to limit the size of their fleets.
September/October, the Chanak crisis.
October, Lloyd George resigned: Bonar Law became PM.
October, Mussolini seized power in Italy.

1923   January, French and Belgium troops occupied the Ruhr.
May, resignation of Bonar Law. Baldwin became PM.
July, Treaty of Lausanne (with Turkey).
December, General Election. Labour formed a minority government under Ramsay MacDonald.

1924   February, Britain recognised the Soviet government.
August, Dawes Plan: Reparations reduced.
October, General Election, after the Zinoviev letter. Comfortable Conservative victory. Baldwin became PM.

1925   October, Locarno Conference: Germany accepted her western borders.

1926   September, Germany joined the League of Nations.
November, Empire Conference in London: the Balfour Declaration: Britain accepted that the Dominions were (essentially) independent.

1927   May, Britain broke off diplomatic relations with Russia after the Arcos affair.

1928   August, the Kellogg-Briand Pact: most of the world's major powers renounced the use of war as an instrument of policy.

1929   May, General Election, resulted in the second minority Labour government under Ramsay MacDonald.

August, the Young Plan extended the period of reparations payment.

October, Anglo-Russian relations resumed.

October, the Wall Street (New York stock market) Crash.

1930　April, Naval Agreement between USA, Britain and Japan.

November, start of first Round Table Conference on India.

1931　January, the Statute of Westminster recognised Dominion independence.

August, National Government formed in Britain.

September, Second Round Table Conference on India: attended by Gandhi.

September, Japanese troops begin military operations in Manchuria.

October, General Election, amidst an atmosphere of economic panic. Overwhelming victory for the National Government.

1932　February, World Disarmament Conference at Geneva.

February, Britain introduces Import Duties Act: end of free trade.

June/July, the Lausanne Conference: end of Reparations.

July/August, Ottawa Economic Conference: Imperial preference.

October, Lord Lytton's Commission reported on the situation in Manchuria.

1933　January, Hitler became Chancellor in Germany.

October, Germany left the Disarmament Conference and the League of Nations.

1934　July, Nazis attempted to seize power in Austria: Chancellor Dollfuss murdered.

1935　March, Hitler announced German rearmament.

April, the Stresa Front: Britain, France and Italy combined against Germany.

June, Baldwin took over as PM from MacDonald.

June, Anglo-German Naval Agreement.

August, the Government of India act passed.

October, Italy invaded Abyssinia.

November, the League applied economic sanctions against Italy.

November, Baldwin's National Government won the General Election.

December, the Hoare-Laval Plan. Resignation of Hoare. Eden became Foreign Secretary.

1936　March, German troops re-occupied the Rhineland.

May, Abyssinia became part of the Italian Empire.

July, start of the Spanish Civil War.

1937　April, new Indian Constitution came into force.

May, Neville Chamberlain replaced Baldwin as PM.

July, Chinese-Japanese war.

November, Lord Halifax visited Hitler.

1938 February, Eden resigned as Foreign Secretary: replaced by Halifax.

March, the Anschluss: Hitler annexed Austria.

August, Lord Runciman's mission to Czechoslovakia.

15 September, Chamberlain met Hitler at Berchtesgaden.

22–23 September, Chamberlain met Hitler at Godesberg.

29–30 September, the Munich Conference.

1939 January, Chamberlain and Halifax visited Italy.

March, the end of Czechoslovakia.

March, Memel returned to Germany by Lithuania.

March, British guarantee to Poland.

April, Britain introduced conscription.

May, the Pact of Steel between Germany and Italy.

August, the Nazi-Soviet Pact.

1 September, Germany invaded Poland.

3 September, Britain and France declared war on Germany.

Acknowledgements

The publishers would like to thank the following for permission to reproduce copyright illustrations:

National Portrait Gallery, London, cover
David Low, Evening Standard/Centre for the Study of Cartoon and Caricature, University of Kent at Canterbury p. 33; p. 77; p. 105
Punch Publications p. 60; p. 108; p. 121

The publishers would like to thank the following for permission to reproduce material in this volume:

Cassell Plc for the extract from *The Gathering Storm*, Winston Churchill (1948); Longman Group UK for the extract *Chamberlain's Birmingham Speech* from *The Origins of the Second World War*, P M H Bell (1986); Methuen & Co for the extract *The 1926 British Foreign Office Memorandum* from *British Foreign Policy Since Versailles*, W N Medlicott (1968); Oxford University Press for the extract *Voight's opinion of Russia* quoted in *The British Press and Germany 1936*, F R Gannon (1971); Princeton University Press for the extract from *The Change in the European Balance of Power, 1938–1939: The Path to Ruin*, Murray, Williamson P159 (1984).

Every effort has been made to trace and acknowledge ownership of copyright. The publishers will be glad to make suitable arrangements with any copyright holders whom it has not been possible to contact.

Index